FINDING THE FRONT DOOR

My Story Of Survival

This story isn't about avoiding your fear.
It's about taking it with you and doing it anyway.

A MEMOIR

BY HJORDIS MADSEN

Author Note:

I would like to give a gentle warning to readers as they venture into this memoir as it contains serious subject matters such as descriptions of attempted murder, domestic violence, sexual assault as well as discussions of sobriety. These subject matters may not be appropriate for all ages. Take care in reading as some subjects may trigger personal experiences in your own lives.

Disclaimer

This memoir is a work of personal reflection based on the author's lived experiences. To protect the privacy of individuals, names have been omitted and replaced with relationship descriptors (such as "my mother," "a friend", "my estranged husband").
All events and accounts are presented as truthfully and accurately as possible, to the best of the author's memory and understanding. However, memory is inherently subjective, and certain details—such as timelines, dialogue, or sequences of events—may have been reconstructed or condensed for clarity and narrative flow.
This work is not intended to defame, misrepresent, or harm any individual. Rather, it is a personal account of survival, growth, and reflection, shared in good faith.

Viking Mama Publishing

DEDICATION

To all who believed in me when I didn't believe in myself. I see you and I love you. To Nick and Christina, there are no words powerful enough. I would do anything to ensure your happiness. I will love you in bad times and in good. Always. Xo

PROLOGUE

"Can we talk?"

Those three words stare up at me from the screen, pulling me toward a rabbit hole I never imagined would find me.

Do I answer her?

My first instinct is to ask, "*What happened?"* but then just as quickly, I tell myself to slow down.

I know writing back is a bad idea. I can't open this can of worms. Not now.

There is nothing good that would come from responding to this message from a stranger.

I found it by accident, buried in my spam folder. It had been sent several months earlier. Why now?

I hover over it for a moment. I don't accept it. I don't delete it. I don't block her. Instead, I slide my phone in my pocket and I go in search of coffee. I try to push it out of my mind.

It doesn't work.

Standing in my kitchen, staring out into the yard, the past slips from the shadows and wraps itself around my throat. Nearly thirty years peel away without asking permission. I take a sip of coffee, holding my cup a little tighter than usual as I try to slow my racing heart.

Memories begin to surface from a life I have tried to escape from.

Outside, Vinnie, our German Shepherd, circles his dog run, nose pressed into the grass. I hate he's out there on the dog run and not inside with me, but that had not been my idea.

I stand at the kitchen window, my hands wrapped around a

cup of fresh brewed coffee. I take a timid sip and I remind myself to let him inside afterward. To feed him.

To keep moving through the small routines that make a day feel ordinary.

But first, I need a shower.

There's a lot to do today. Packing boxes and bags of clothes litter the bedroom. The rest isn't going to pack itself.

I strip down and climb over the tub, twisting the knobs until water crashes over my bare skin. I close my eyes and push my hair back, letting it soak completely as steam begins to curl around me.

Today is a big day. It's moving day.

Today, I am leaving my husband of almost four years. Together for almost six. I am ending a relationship that has reshaped me in ways I still have no language for.

Today, I close this chapter of my life.

Today, his manipulation ends.

CHAPTER 1

Filling Clothes Into Bags

Lost in thought, I kept moving.

I'm filling clothes into bags.

When he walked into the room, my back was to the door. I didn't hear him come in. He moved quietly.

Almost like a sleek cat, trying to avoid detection.

Like a panther out in the wild, hidden in the dark, lurking in shadows, preparing to strike.

The room was dark, illuminated by nothing more than a small table lamp.

Maybe two table lamps.

It was dim and deliberate, creating pockets of shadow and silence, as though the room was set for a scene in a movie – inviting me in while quietly warning me to pay attention.

I didn't know he was behind me.

But then, I felt him. His arms wrapped around me from behind, pinning both of my arms tightly to my sides.

The shirts in my hands fell to the floor. For a split second, I was confused. I tried to pull away.

He tightened his grip.

What the hell are you doing?

Let me go!

I struggled, twisting my body, trying to free my arms. My mind raced. I just needed to think.

Think.

And, quickly!

What is happening right now?

Why wouldn't he just let go of me?

"Let me go! Let me go now!"

The voice coming out of me didn’t sound like mine.

Suddenly the room tilted. My body hit the floor, his weight crushing down on top of me.

Then his hands moved.

Fast.

His fingers locked around my throat.

He squeezed.

And, then the ceiling blurred.

CHAPTER 2

Why Did It Take Me This Long?

It's a quiet, hot night.

No stars above, just haze from the heatwave the Pacific Northwest is having. I'm on our back porch, half-naked, sprawled across the L-shaped bench, shifting cushions until my body settles into something that resembles being comfortable.

I stretch my legs out groaning as my muscles ache. My right elbow props me up just enough to hold my phone, open Google Docs and start a new chapter.

It hurts everywhere before I even type the first word.

I blame him.

Midnight just passed.

It's officially twenty-five years since he tried to kill me.

Even now, certain sounds split my body open before my brain can catch up.

A man's voice rises from somewhere behind my eyes, *"today you are going to die…to die…"*

The visions seep in. I see him. I see myself. I want to believe we were different people then. I know I am now.

The porch is quiet except for Alexa playing a few of my favorite country songs. But the noise rising inside me gets louder by the minute. I want to scream from some hollow place buried deep inside me. I want to sob for every painful memory that day left me with.

I want to punch a wall. Run five miles. Dance to something loud and reckless. Stay awake for days. Eat garbage. Drink until the feeling disappears.

Skip showers for a week. Sleep all day long. Clean obsessively. Vacuum twice a day. Drink two pots of coffee in two hours. Fly to the moon. Disappear inside a blanket fort.

Go shopping for shit I don't need.

I want to be anywhere but here, carrying the pain gifted to me twenty-five years ago.

Sometimes I wonder what he did with his life afterward. I know enough. And, I totally question my desire to even know anything about him.

He isn't worth my time.

He isn't worth a thought.

But an apology would be nice.

Some acknowledgment that he is not the man I last saw.

Some remorse for fucking up my internal dialogue that still bends around him.

Some apology for flinching when anything comes near my neck.

For sleeping with dim lights scattered in my bedroom. For making me hate guns.

Pain ignores calendars. Trauma could not care less what your plans are.

We forget long enough to build lives — raising kids, hosting dinners, closing business deals, laughing with friends — carefully packing skeletons into closets we promise never to open again.

We try to lean into everything good. We forget for a while and move through the world as if the devil hadn't shown up wearing a familiar face.

"You've ruined my life. Now, I am going to ruin yours..."

Until the door refuses to stay shut.

Two years ago, mine blew open.

It was time to drag the memory into the daylight. It was time to stop leaving lights on in every room of the house. It's time to feel it. Study it from above before stepping back inside it. Time to take my life apart piece by piece and try to understand how it was built in the first place.

I knew the puzzle would never go back together.

I am not that girl. I am not that woman.

I am someone who learned she carries a frightening amount of courage and strength. Giving up was never an option. It still isn't.

When the clock strikes seven in a few hours, I hope I'll be sleeping peacefully in my bed. By eight fifteen, I should be out of the woods – the same minute I found the front door and escaped.

And honestly, I hate that these numbers still haunt me.

No more.

He did what he did.

I survived.

I won.

End of story.

I have to stop searching for answers that don't exist.

Stop letting questions live rent-free inside my head.

I'm going to lie in the kiddie pool in our backyard now.

Let cold water rinse this date off my skin. Pretend it can carry the memory somewhere far away.

It isn't flying to the moon. But it will do.

CHAPTER 3

When At First You Don't Succeed

It was the fall of 2020, and I was stuck – functioning well enough to fool most people, but not myself.

I smiled, laughed, showed up, and did all the right things while my heart felt utterly disengaged from who I was as a human being.

The feeling was both foreign and deeply familiar, like meeting a stranger who somehow knows all your secrets.

I was uncomfortable in my own skin.

My heart had gone quiet.

It didn't seem to care much about anything anymore. The person I cared least about was myself.

I was a middle-aged woman approaching fifty like a rapid-fire meteor shower – moving fast, burning hot, and falling with no clear idea of where I would land.

Impact felt inevitable.

There were no lighthouses guiding me to shore, no warnings steering me away from the rocks. I was suspended in descent, all controls lost, the signal to the mothership gone. Houston, it seemed, had failed this re-entry back to Earth.

What made it unbearable wasn't the falling—it was not understanding *why* I was falling.

If I could name my fears, identify my weaknesses, I believed—deep down—I could find the yellow brick road back to a life that I could recognize. A life that would feel familiar. Maybe even simple and mundane. I would have taken it gladly.

I wanted to laugh and mean it.

Cry without apology.

Yell when someone crossed a line.

I wanted some portion of my confidence back and I wanted to

stop seeing the woman in the mirror as less, simply because she looked tired and sad.

Feeling lost is never about one single thing. It is an accumulation.

My mind has always worked a little differently – either that, or most people don't admit how many tabs are open at once. Mine are always running. Not with the everyday nonsense we all endure, but with the deeper questions: the meaning, the point, the cost of the journey, and the pain we carry along the way.

I want you, my reader, to know that this isn't about living in the past. It's about understanding how deeply the past shapes the people we become, never mind how much of a cliche that is.

This book is more than twenty-five years in the making. I've learned that peeling back one layer of the onion only reveals another beneath it. Human beings are complex beyond measure.

Our layers shift and churn like waves breaking quietly against the sand—sometimes leaving something behind, sometimes taking something with it.

My story is an invitation to better understand the things we are left with and the things that are taken from us.

It's important for me that you, my reader, also know that I am a mother today. Because this story flickers between past and present, it became something I needed to share early on.

Spoiler alert.

It is obvious that I am alive and I did in fact find the front door.

My kids are grown now, and I'll share more about them as we peel the onion together. For clarity, my children came from my second marriage. Although that relationship also ended in divorce, their father has always been very involved in their lives and is a devoted dad. Now that we've set a few important markers along the path, it's time to dive in.

Join me on this chaotic, beautiful, and sometimes sinister journey of uncovering all the pebbles in the sand.

Join me in reckoning with every choice, every heartbreak,

every naked dance in the backyard when it rains.

This is a story about growth – about not always being polite or positive, about shutting people out and letting the right ones in.

About allowing yourself to be who you always were.

And, finally, about not giving a shit what anyone else thinks.

I am not a perfect human. No one is.

I have been treated badly, and I have also treated others badly. I am filled with shortcomings. Remove the rose-colored glasses that often accompany survivors.

This is not a memoir in which I will paint a pretty picture as to the person I have been. It is, however, a memoir that only wishes to focus on one thing – the truth.

For most of us, this is hard.

Judgment comes in quiet, familiar ways—in the look someone gives you from across the room, in the raised eyebrow that questions your autonomy without saying a word. Judgment can leave you gutted and afraid.

This story isn't about avoiding that fear.

It's about taking it with you and doing it anyway.

CHAPTER 4

The Haircut

I sat down tentatively in the chair. Soon a black drape was placed over my body. After some back and forth, I made the decision.

She guided me to the hair washing station and started to massage a beautiful scent of clean, fresh and citrus smelling shampoo into my hair. It had a scent of floral under tones, yet I can't decide what it is exactly.

My eyes flickered shut and I took a deep breath. I quietly smiled to no one in particular and sank deeper into the chair, letting my head fall deeper into the basin and her capable hands.

This was glorious.

The tension in my shoulders slowly escaped through the morning air as she washed my hair. She expertly pushed strong fingers all over my scalp. Shampoo turned into a beautiful lather of suds and soon hot water rinsed the dust of yesterday down the drain.

That was followed by a gentle massage of applying conditioner into my long blond locks. I could literally moan from the pleasure of it all, yet thought better of it.

After a quick towel dry of my hair, we walked together back to her station. I sank yet again into the chair.

It was now or never.

If I didn't want to do this, I had to speak up at that moment.

I had been told my hair was my best feature so many times that it felt less like mine and more like a responsibility.

I remained silent and watched in amazement as clever trained hands clipped long locks of blonde hair away.

They fell to the floor almost as if dancing and landed without a sound around the hairdresser's feet. It all seemed so simple.

Years of holding on to something so beautiful, was clipped away in an instant.

Snip.

My wedding day.

Snip. His hand touching my hair in passing.

Snip. Silence.

Just silence.

I felt a sense of unease but I pressed it down like a good little girl. I was a good girl. But not at this moment. He wouldn't think so. I inhale and look at myself in the large mirror.

Pure excitement surfaced on my face as she added product to my hair loosely running her fingers through the hair that remained. She moved quickly as she pushed it to this side and that side as she continued styling.

I looked at myself in amazement when she was finished. A new sense of authority washed over me.

I didn't feel fearless.

I felt… tentative.

Like someone trying on courage for the first time.

Taking charge of this little thing would mean I could soon take control of other, more important matters in my life.

Leaving the salon, there was a new pep in my step as my boots clicked loudly on the tiled floor. As the automatic doors open, a rush of stagnant air greets me. I clutch my keys as I take another deep breath, trying to remain excited and to push away any doubt I may be feeling.

It wasn't doubt I was pushing away.

It was a rehearsal for what was coming next.

Making my way to my car, I pushed my shoulders back and stood up taller as I placed one foot in front of the other, growing more confident with each step. My legs felt strong and determined as I made my way through the busy parking lot. They were not buckling under the pressure I could feel just under the surface of my skin.

"Had I really done this?"

I think to myself in disbelief suddenly.

This was a freedom that felt unfamiliar and it was pure, silly, empowering and frightening all at the same time.

The drive home was quick and as I opened the front door, there he was.

I was hoping he would be there to see it.

To witness this new version of me that had come to life.

I had been gaining confidence each time short tendrils of hair danced around my face, framing it, as the wind hit it through the open car window on the way here.

He stood there in the center of our living room, rushing towards the front door as if he was heading somewhere.

Then he stopped and all I could hear was a quick inhale of breath coming from him. His grip tightened around the keys in his hand and I could see his knuckles were turning white.

All at once, I could see realization connect the dots from what he was looking at and who was standing in front of him.

A young girl, barely twenty-three, wearing skin tight jeans, a loose fitting t-shirt, black boots and a faded denim jacket with large silver buttons. Just standing there, momentarily frozen to the spot, waiting, I felt a sense of dread as his eyes connected with mine.

He didn't disappoint.

Perhaps, I had wanted to test him slightly. To see if the mask would come off or if he would be capable of hiding his true feelings in order to actually support my decision. Because ultimately it had been MY decision to cut my hair short.

That was my right. His input would be important to a degree, but this was all up to me, is what I had told myself.

I am young and fun, I am a business owner and I have things to do. That requires a serious haircut, I decided.

Or did I hear that in a movie? Doesn't matter.

Just then as he opened his mouth to speak, a sharp pain traveled through me as if to warn off what was coming.

"What the fuck did you do to your hair? You look like a boy

and you're fucking ugly now..." his voice loomed big in the short distance between us.

Tears loomed in my eyes and I struggled to hold them at bay. I wouldn't let him see the pain his words had delivered.

I took a step towards him, *"I like it and that's all that matters. It's my hair."* I walked around him and down the hall to my home office, closing the door. Soon after, I heard the front door slam and he was gone.

Well, that wasn't so hard now was it? It turns out, the real thing I had cut away wasn't my hair.

CHAPTER 5

Intersection

When I was a little girl, life seemed simpler.

It wasn't.

I was a generally happy child, but there was a sadness in me too—the kind you can't quite name, only feel. It lingered just beneath the surface, ready to rise at any moment.

It reminds me now of standing in a crowded room as an adult, surrounded by people, yet feeling completely alone. Back then I didn't have the words for it, but maybe it was the feeling of always being on the outside looking in. As if I had arrived in the wrong era, the wrong story. As if this wasn't the life I was meant to step into.

I don't say this to wound anyone; it isn't directed at a single soul. I love my family. I loved them more because so many of the key players left my life too soon. They died. But to a child, death feels the same as leaving—and the silence afterward feels the same too.

What I also didn't know then was just how deeply it would shape my adult life—this notion of people leaving. And what grows beside that notion is almost predictable.

Loving someone becomes complicated.

Love is a quiet exchange of give and take.

There are moments when your own needs and wants slip to the side, not because they disappear, but because their happiness begins to feel tied to your own.

No matter how deeply you care, there's that silent fear whispering that they too might one day leave. This is such a hard truth to carry. It makes you wonder, at times, why anyone would risk loving at all.

Why open your heart when loss feels like the unspoken cost of admission? Because the pain associated with losing that same love, can't be measured. It pulls you into deep and dark spaces. So, why choose love? Why take a chance on something so powerful as love, when there is so much pain that comes with it when it sours?

Because sometimes you don't have a choice. We are programmed to love other people. Our parents, our siblings, our husbands and wives and our children. When we lose them, we lose a part of ourselves.

I have lost many tiny pieces of myself over the years, because of love. And, guess what?

That is ok. No matter the pain it created, I know that I have loved and been loved. That is the greatest feeling on earth. Nobody can ever take that feeling away from you once you've known it. This is why we continue to love, because it's magical. It can be beautiful.

Knowing where to begin a story is always the hardest part. It seems obvious to start at the beginning, but sometimes the beginning doesn't make sense until much later – after you've lived a little.

While we're in the middle of our own lives, we rarely see clearly. Part of us lives in a carefully constructed world where the truth sits somewhere in between reality and what we can bear to believe. The version of truth we can survive at the time. So maybe I only saw what I was capable of understanding then. Maybe the rest had to wait for a future version of me to be ready. Like I said – some beginnings only reveal themselves years later.

The beginning of where to begin my story revealed itself unexpectedly. I was sitting at a red light enroute to yet another client. I was dreading it as I had many other times as of late. Here I was, a forty-something year old woman, cleaning houses for a living.

I never in my wildest childhood dreams imagined this for my life. Even so, I never did let my work define me. We are not what we do for a living.

Yet, it felt as if I was spinning my wheels at times, putting one foot in front of the other.

Some days I found myself taking two steps back. Some days,

four steps forward. It was decent money. I provided for my family. Some weeks were better than others, yet I always played the math game in my head while running the vacuum over countless floors.

How many more floors this week to pay the bills?

So, there I was at that intersection. An intersection in the road; yet it might as well have been the most perfect symbol for my life. I was completely lost in thought. The music was playing so loud I found myself in another dimension. A different time and space.

Other drivers were speeding by yet I was seeing them as if in slow motion. It was then I knew. My life was passing me by, and it was time for me to step out of my large, yet comfortable box.

It was time to at least open the door to something different. Something so frightening, it would take a small miracle for me to take that leap.

And although that was the beginning of traveling back in time, it turns out it would still take over ten years to complete it.

CHAPTER 6

Just An Unassuming Day

It was an early summer morning near the end of June. Next month I will be celebrating my twenty-fourth birthday.

The Pacific Northwest felt deceptively calm and warm. Sunlight slipped through the windows as if nothing in the world was wrong. The sky carried a clean tint of blue. It felt like it was going to be an unassuming kind of day. The kind that doesn't announce itself. The kind that doesn't warn you.

At first glance, it felt as if the day intended to pass without consequence. I needed it to go well.

My life, though, was anything but calm. Uncertainty and chaos lived just beneath the surface. Most people couldn't see it. We rarely show the parts that are unraveling. But I was living right in the middle of a quiet disaster – chaos invisible to an unsuspecting passerby.

Coffee in hand, I stood at the kitchen window and looked into the backyard. Vinnie, my German Shepherd, paced along the dog run in the backyard. Nose low. Ears alert. He lifted his head once, staring toward the house.

I didn't recognize the tension in his body. Animals know before we do.

Later, he would bark until his throat gave out. He would throw himself against that line, desperate to get to me.

The restraint I once resented would keep him alive.

I watched him for a moment longer than usual.

If I had known, I would have watched him longer.

Vinnie had been my husband's answer when I asked about having children. I wouldn't understand that until months later, when friends gently pointed it out. I had been so blind. Until I wasn't.

Vinnie was beautiful - traditional German Shepherd coloring. He reminded me of my childhood dog, Tell. At least, that's how I chose to see him. We used to walk every evening to the makeshift off-leash park fifteen minutes from our house. It had been our routine.

We used to look like a couple building a life.

That was before clarity. Before truth began separating itself from lies.

At 6:30 a.m., I stood in the shower. The steady rhythm of hot water was the only sound. I was in a temporary shelter from my thoughts. Outside, summer carried on, indifferent to my life.

The world was unaware. So was I.

I didn't yet understand that this stillness was not peace – but a pause.

For a few suspended minutes, I felt alone in the safest way. I didn't know it was the last peaceful moment of my old life. Stillness can be deceptive. It often arrives right before impact.

How could I have known? There's no use inserting what-ifs here. Life happens. Sometimes we are simply along for the ride.

It all began with that shower.

My eyes were closed. Water cascading over my body. My thoughts — usually loud, relentless — quieted.

Soap slid across my legs, my thighs, my stomach. My hands are familiar. Gentle. Grounding.

I remember my flat stomach. Years later I would smile softly at that memory, noticing stretch marks and softness where that smoothness once lived.

I cupped my breast to lather more soap and inhaled deeply. Chamomile body wash mixed with steam, filling our small bathroom with a scent that felt like luxury.

I felt beautiful.

I felt hopeful.

My life was moving forward. I believed it was about to get better.

It was meditation before meditation was fashionable. Hot yoga before anyone was calling it that. It was simply a young woman standing in her own body, believing she had time.

I didn't.

Peace, I would later learn, is sometimes just a brief mercy. And it would not last.

That freshness. That peace.

It would be torn down.

Bruised.

Splattered with blood.

My blood.

What a waste of good body wash.

Later that day, I would take another shower. That one would be different.

There would be no calm.

No centering.

Only shock.

Only the slow realization that nothing would ever be the same again.

I should have been alarmed by the sudden thud — maybe it was a door. I heard it just as I was finishing. I pushed the curtain aside.

"Hello? Who's there?"

No reply.

Probably one of the cats jumping from the counter.

I finished, dried off, pulled on gray sweatpants and a white tank top.

After towel drying my hair, I decided to go grab the newspaper from our mailbox across the street.

One of my wedding portraits was on the front of the Bridal Registry. A small triumph.

Proof that I was building something of my own. Through connections with the Norwegian American Chamber of Commerce, a reporter had featured my work.

I started in photography at sixteen as an assistant. By nineteen, after two years of college, I launched my own wedding photography business.

Weddings. White dresses. First kisses. Promises spoken in sunlight. I was young, ambitious, and relentless.

And naïve.

What nineteen year old isn't a little naive? Wisdom comes as we move through life. We can't know until life gives us time and experience.

At twenty-three, clarity was beginning to edge its way in. Not everyone in my life wanted me to succeed. Someone was determined to keep me small. To keep me uncertain. Someone was intent on preventing the emotional maturity I was just beginning to find.

That someone was my estranged husband.

And today, I was leaving.

I had made the decision. I had found a place. I had gathered my courage in quiet pieces.

This was supposed to be the first morning of the rest of my life.

Instead, it would be the last morning of who I used to be.

But first, I had to cross the street.

And get the newspaper.

CHAPTER 7

They Chose To Keep Me

My mother was diagnosed with leukemia around the same time my parents learned they were expecting their fourth child — me.

Much of what I know about that time was told to me later, usually by my father.

As a young child, I often woke in the middle of the night from shapeless nightmares I could never fully explain. Many nights, I dreamt that I had died. I would crawl downstairs and find my dad sitting in the living room. I would climb into his lap, and he would calm me with stories.

Stories about how he met my mother while working as a Merchant Marine on a massive ship that traveled the world. I remember, even at five or six years old, feeling an urgency to pay attention. To memorize what he was telling me. As if some quiet instinct knew I would need these stories later.

He had left his homeland of Denmark at fifteen, finding work at sea, carrying goods from port to port. The world opened to him that way — one shoreline at a time.

Years later, I would follow a similar path. Just before turning sixteen, I left my own homeland. I made my way to the United States, where I have lived ever since.

My father met my mother a few years after joining the Merchant Marines. She was the Captain's only daughter — the only daughter of the man who would later become my grandfather. I never did meet him or my grandmother as they died before and/or shortly after my birth.

After what appears to have been a brief courtship, my parents married and settled in a small seaside town in Norway, about an hour from the capital. This is where I grew up. The kind of town where everyone knew everyone.

My brother came first. Then my sister. Then another brother. I was born ten years later— the fourth child, the baby. The three of them were only about four years apart. My mother had three children in the span of roughly four years.

I often think about that now. The diapers. The exhaustion. The noise. She must have been extraordinary. Something tells me she was.

So, ten years after her youngest child, I was due to arrive. And, my beginning did not come easily.

In 1972, when leukemia was far less understood — especially in Norway — doctors advised my parents to consider terminating the pregnancy because of my mother's diagnosis.

They chose not to.

They chose me.

I suspect my mother was not fully told how severe her illness was. That it was terminal.

But she must have known something. She was only thirty-two.

That has always been difficult for me.

You could call it survivor's guilt. I lived. She died. My birth marks the beginning of their loss. I have often felt — irrationally, but persistently — that I stole something from my siblings. Their childhood. Their mother. The fierce protection and love she gave them.

When I sit with that thought, I have to let it hang in the air. As she was dying, I was living.

I also stole something from my father. His beautiful wife. His forever love. And yet, not once did he show me resentment. He wrapped me with love. Unspoken mostly as most vikings keep their feelings wrapped up tightly. I felt it though.

Always.

According to my father, I was their love child. They had tried for years to have another baby. Some distant relatives suggested I was an afterthought. That angered my father deeply. He was protective that way.

He made sure I knew I was wanted. Chosen. Loved.

After my mother died — when I was only one month and three days old — he tried, in his way, to be both parents.

My older sister stepped in too. She pushed me in my stroller to meet her friends. Took me to the beach. Sang in cars to country music. Took me on long drives between Norway and Denmark to visit our grandmother - our dad's mom - when I was older. She mothered me the best she could. Her sacrifices went above and beyond. I'll always be grateful for that.

Our father died just before I turned thirteen.

After that, I went to live with my sister, her husband, and their son. But when my father died, it felt as though he took a piece of me with him — one I would never get back. He had been larger than life to me. Losing him felt like losing gravity.

All of this is to say: my story began unevenly.

And the man who would later become my husband understood that imbalance.

He had no interest in helping me heal from childhood grief. Instead, he studied it. He learned where the wounds were and pressed on them. He used the loss of my parents as leverage – twisting my sorrow into something shameful, something weak.

When I shared those losses with him, I did so from trust. I believed vulnerability would be met with care, not weaponized.

It wasn't.

Some people say showing sadness is a sign of weakness. I know better. To feel—to allow yourself to feel anything at all—takes tremendous strength. It is far easier to push pain aside, to pretend it doesn't matter, to build walls and call them protection. Facing real emotion is heavy.

It is painful.

Love and loss are painful.

Did I miss them?

Every single day.

I missed the moments that never became memories. The ordinary conversations most people take for granted. I missed the questions I never had the chance to ask.

I have learned that grief is rarely loud.

It doesn't always fill the room with resounding sobbing cries.

More often, grief lives quietly. It lingers in the space behind closed doors. It sits in the empty chair. It follows you from year to year.

Sometimes grief is simply the weight of what never was — carried without ceremony, without witnesses, but always there.

The man I would marry chose to witness my grief.

And then he pivoted, wrapped his hands around my throat, and used it against me. *"You miss your parents so much,"* he said.

"Today, you're going to see them again."

CHAPTER 8

What Did He Just Say?

When I opened the front door and made the quick jaunt to the end of the driveway, I saw him. I was not expecting to see him before 7 a.m.

A sense of dread started to build. Quietly. Not enough for me to give it real attention. He hadn't told me he planned to be there that morning.

My estranged husband stood next to the car parked on the street – his father's car. Why was he not driving one of his own cars?

He had moved in with his parents two weeks earlier. It was temporary. Until I moved out.

Today was that day.

Annoyance slipped into my voice.

"What are you doing here? You're supposed to be at work in less than an hour."

He smiled and didn't appear to notice my clipped tone.

"Your portraits came out today in the newspaper. I wanted to bring you a copy," he answered.

I grabbed the paper and started walking back towards the house. He followed me. He may have even asked if he could come in. I might have muttered something in response. I don't remember clearly. I left him to his own devices and continued with my plans for the day.

I walked straight into the bedroom and began pulling clothes from the closet shelves. A black garbage bag was at my feet and I kept throwing clothes into it. Armful after armful of shirts, jeans, sweaters.

"I really must donate some of these clothes," I thought to myself.

"There's too much here for one person."

Once at my new apartment, I would sort everything. Keep what mattered. Let the rest go.

Sitting here now, almost thirty years later, the memory of this detail throws me. Maybe it's a self preservation mechanism. Our brains only allow so much to remain, before it fractures the rest.

If that's true, I wish it had erased the next hour and fifteen minutes instead. As much as I've put this behind me, I know, the images of that day will truly never completely disappear.

What happened next was not impulsive. Nor was it a casual attempt to scare me. It was deliberate.

Planned.

I saw it in his eyes.

I should have run.

But I am getting ahead of myself.

Lost in thought, I kept moving. Filling clothes into bags. When he walked into the room, my back was to the door. I didn't hear him come in.

He moved quietly.

Almost like a sleek cat, trying to avoid detection. Like a panther out in the wild, hidden in the dark, lurking in shadows, preparing to strike.

The room was dark, illuminated by nothing more than a small table lamp. Maybe two table lamps. It was dim and deliberate, creating pockets of shadow and silence, as though the room was set for a scene in a movie – inviting me in while quietly warning me to pay attention.

I didn't know he was behind me.

But then, I felt him. His arms wrapped around me from behind, pinning both of my arms tightly to my sides.

The shirts in my hands fell to the floor. For a split second, I was confused. I tried to pull away. He tightened his grip.

"What the hell are you doing? Let me go!" I say internally.

I struggled, twisting my body, trying to free my arms. My mind raced. I just needed to think.

Think. And, quickly!

What is happening right now? Why wouldn't he just let go of me?

"Let me go! Let me go now!"

The voice coming out of me didn't sound like mine.

Suddenly the room tilted. My body hit the floor, his weight crushing down on top of me.

Then his hands moved. Fast.

His fingers locked around my throat. He squeezed. And, then the ceiling blurred.

I tried to inhale but nothing came. My head thrashed from side to side as I clawed at his wrists. My legs kicked wildly. I tried to roll. I tried to crawl. I tried to stand. My nails dug into his skin. He didn't loosen his grip.

My mind was trying to understand. But my body took over instead.

Air.

I need air.

My lungs expanded automatically, desperate for oxygen, but nothing came in. It felt as if a door had slammed shut inside my throat. My mouth opened wide, pulling, searching.

Nothing.

A sharp buzzing filled my ears. I could hear my own heartbeat so loudly it drowned out everything else. My hands kept pulling at his wrists. I didn't have time to make a plan – it was a reaction.

Not strategic – primal.

I twisted my body violently, trying to throw him off balance. My legs kicked, heel slamming into the floor, into the closet doors, into anything. It was not graceful. I became an animal fighting for survival.

His grip tightened. Black spots swarmed the edges of my vision, closing in like a narrowing tunnel. His dark eyes bore into mine. They had turned black as coal. My head felt heavy and light at the same time. My face burned and my chest convulsed, trying to inhale.

I needed air.

Air.

Air.

Air.

The brain does not think clearly when oxygen disappears. It does not negotiate. There is no reasoning. It fights however.

I bucked my hips upward, trying to get away from him. I twisted sideways, forcing both of us to roll. For a split second, his balance shifted.

The split second saved me.

For now.

One of my hands slipped between his wrist and my throat – barely – just enough to create the smallest gap.

A thin, ragged gasp tore into my lungs.

It hurt. It burned. But it was air. My body surged with it.

Adrenaline flooded through me and it was hot and electric. My arms suddenly felt stronger than they ever had before. I clawed, shoved, twisted again. My elbow connected with something solid – maybe it was his leg or maybe it was the edge of the nightstand where the home telephone sat.

He faltered briefly, but it was all I needed. Survival is neither elegant nor pretty. Pride or dignity are lost causes. It only cares about one thing. Staying alive.

His voice cut through the chaos again. It was deliberate and unfamiliar.

The threat kept playing on repeat, over and over, louder than my thoughts, louder than the panic clawing its way in.

"Today... you're going to die... to die... to die..."

I immediately felt a shift inside me. No.

Not today.

Not like this.

"You miss your parents so much," he said.

"Well, today you're going to see them again. Because today...you're going to die."

Die.

Die.

Die.

Somewhere beneath the pounding in my ears and the fire in my lungs, another voice rose up.

Not today.

CHAPTER 9

February Third, 1992

"I received a letter the other day filled with pictures of my brother and sister-in-law, and the children too of course. They are so cute. I wish I could go see them one of these days.

Amongst the happy photographs, there was yet another photo that brought with it happy and sad memories. It was a picture of my parents' grave. It was decorated with Christmas wreaths and shining lights.

The vision kind of stayed on my mind long after I had put the photos aside. I remembered a time so long ago when tears were never far away. I remember times when I would sit at their grave and cry so hard and so long. The feelings inside me would flow out and keep going until I felt utterly and completely empty.

I needed those moments and I recall them cleansing my soul so I could go on with my life; at least for a while, before I would return some time later to let go of my feelings all over again.

I suppose I enjoy those memories and will never let them die. You see, if I allow the memories to die, to fade, it would be as if I was letting them (actually) die and never be remembered again."

This was a journal entry written by a girl I no longer recognize. I was young and I was broken. Grief was so familiar, I didn't know how to let it go. When I shared my pain, I was looking for a lifeline.

Someone to understand and validate me.

Someone to tell me that there was nothing wrong with me for feeling lost. My younger self needed guidance.

Instruction. Understanding. Grace.

My younger self didn't need control.

Coercion.

Cruelty.

I needed a partner, an equal, to help me grow as a person and to help me move through my grief.

Walk beside me as I was striving to find the emotional maturity I needed. He didn't do that.

Instead of seeing me, truly seeing me, he used it against me to make me feel small and insignificant.

"I loved them so, my mother and my father," the journal entry continues.

"*They gave me life and the opportunity to live. I need not ask why they left me so soon anymore because there will never be an answer. There will never be an answer to the fact that they died and left me all alone.*

Let me talk about something else. You know how much death frightens me sometimes and almost chokes me. Let me talk about love.

There are several kinds of love; there is the one children receive from their parents, the one siblings give each other. There is the one between good, special friends and then finally there is the love between a woman and a man.

I love him so much. I love his gentle ways of life, his ambitious strive to succeed, his loving smile and passionate kisses.

Where did I ever find and capture him? I am to be his wife soon. In about four months. In many ways I'm excited, but I'm also scared.

Will things change once we are married, I wonder?

There is one thing I know that will never change; our love for each other. It has grown faithfully every day since we met. I fear not that it will fade; ever!

He sleeps so quietly; his breathing only a soft noise in my ear, that I can hardly hear him.

Every night I lay next to him and hold him close. I will never let him go because I need him so much. I love him far too much to ever let him go without a fight."

We would eventually fight. Not the kind this journal entry implies however.

He wouldn't be fighting to save a marriage.

He would be fighting to end me.

CHAPTER 10

The Wedding Dress

I hadn't planned for it to happen this way, but there I was, standing alone in the middle of a bridal boutique. With my purse slung over my shoulder, I hesitated, overwhelmed before I had even touched a single dress. I was getting married in just a few short months.

I let that reality settle as I stared at the gowns displayed around me. Satin and tulle shimmered beneath soft lighting. Rhinestones and pearls caught every flicker of movement. Every shade of white and ivory hung in careful rows. Some dresses carried long dramatic trains, others were short or sleek. A few were so full a woman could disappear inside the layers of fabric.

A saleswoman approached and asked if I needed help. I told her I was just looking, but she gently took charge anyway, offering to prepare a fitting room. I agreed. Before long, several dresses were waiting for me.

I wished I hadn't come alone. It would have been nice to have girlfriends there. Or better yet, my mother.

Sadness pressed into my chest for a moment.

This was one of those milestones every girl imagines sharing with her mother, and that would never be part of my story.

"Why did I come alone?"

I pushed the thought aside and stepped into the dressing room.

"I've got this," I told myself.

It was just a dress.

As I removed my jeans and top, then slipped the first dress on, I could hear the soft muffled conversations of another bride there to do exactly as I was. The store wasn't crowded, yet hearing the giggles and excited exclamations as one woman showed off her choice to the women with her, it made me flinch a little on the inside.

When the saleswoman zipped the final inches and I turned toward the mirror, I knew. This was the one.

I said yes to the dress before that became a thing.

Not in front of friends, a mother, a sister or bridesmaids, just a stranger who was doing her job.

It fit me like a glove and would only need a few minor alterations to tighten up the off the shoulder bodice. Pearls gleamed from every direction and lace adorned the outer edges of the large train. It complimented my thin waist and then poofed out just perfectly at my hips.

I touched the satin fabric and felt like an absolute princess.

I shyly kept staring at myself in the mirror, just for a moment, wondering who this girl was. As I dreamt of how I would style my hair and what shoes to pick later, yet somewhere in the back of my mind, the question lingered-why had I come alone?

Today, I know why.

Isn't it funny how after decades of living and observing, it doesn't seem so out of focus? Where before the aperture was slightly off, now everything becomes crystal clear. I simply needed a sharper camera lens or better yet, a better technique in framing the photograph.

There wasn't anyone to come with me.

Not really.

I didn't have any girlfriends my own age and one of my bridesmaids was flying in with my brother as she was my sister-in-law. It didn't feel like a thing I could do as most things revolved around just him.

Today, I know this should have been something that made me question getting married in the first place.

It feels like it was done on a total whim.

I went into the store, picked one, paid for it and left throwing it over my arm.

As if I had stopped in for a sandwich.

It didn't feel important enough to have people there with me, hence I didn't seek out the few friends I did have.

I was getting married.

I needed a dress.

Done.

CHAPTER 11

The Wedding

I let out a slow breath, lifted the corners of my mouth into a smile, and placed one foot in front of the other.

I was nineteen years old.

I was walking down the aisle on my brother's arm.

He had flown across the Atlantic from Norway to give me away to a man who was thirty-five.

Thirty-five.

Old enough to have lived nearly two of my lifetimes. Old enough to know exactly who he was. I barely knew who I was.

Not me.

Not my brother. Not anyone.

My sister knew.

She wasn't there that day.

Years earlier she had tried to warn me, but at eighteen I played the rebellious card and refused to listen. If only I knew then what I know today.

Life doesn't usually play out like that.

But life has peaks and valleys, and when you're in the valley you rarely know it. Only later do we find understanding.

It was a typical May day in The Pacific Northwest – cool, clouds scattered across the sky over our lakeside venue. As long as it didn't rain.

I woke up as if it was any other wedding day. I was used to weddings. I had photographed dozens, I knew the rhythm - the vows, the kiss, the cake cutting, the bouquet toss.

I was familiar with being behind the camera.

I was unfamiliar with being one of the main characters.

Was I anxious? Were there questions swirling around in my mind? Did I have any thoughts of running?

I honestly don't know.

I do know this – I was nineteen and he was thirty-five, and no one questioned it loudly enough for me to hear.

Walking down the aisle, my eyes scanning people's faces, I smiled. I was calm and happy. There were no alarm bells urging me to pivot and run.

Perhaps a few nervous knocks kicked around in my belly but that's to be expected. I caught him looking at me, with a sheepish grin on his face.

I wonder now what that smile meant. I will never know.

The day went by in a blur.

There were portraits taken. A lot of friends and family. Stunning flower arrangements.

There was a ceremony, yet I have no memory of my vows.

The first kiss. Don't recall that either.

All these years later, it is as if someone erased the film. Or left it too long in the developer and they have faded to white, ghostly images with faint outlines.

There was catered food, friends, and dancing.

There was the cutting of the cake, the bouquet toss and the first dance. All events associated with every wedding I have ever photographed. All vanished from my mind twenty-five years later.

He did make me laugh and he did appear to love me.

The problem was – he loved me in a way that required ownership. A nineteen-year-old does not always recognize possession disguised as protection. A thirty-five-year-old does.

He wanted me all to himself.

He wanted to control my every move.

Who I spoke to, who I met for lunch, who I considered a friend.

"That is not love" I now whisper quietly to myself.

But, as I swayed my hips to the music, these thoughts were the furthest thing from my mind. Surrounded by my new husband – friends and family – dancing the night away, I wasn't scared of the future.

I wasn't scared he would ever hurt me.

I was nineteen while my new husband was thirty-five.

Sparkling cider for me. Beer and wine for everyone else.

We threw one hell of a party.

My inheritance paid for it.

My father funded that wedding from the grave. I sometimes think he would have rolled over six feet under had he known what was coming.

Today, as I write this, it is the anniversary of that date.

Twenty-five years.

The birds are chirping in the late afternoon sun. There is no music today. No cake or fancy flower bouquets to commemorate this anniversary, that was never meant to be. Clearly, this date has no meaning today and I only realized it later in the day – almost as an afterthought.

It means nothing now.

This marriage didn't fail solely because of him. I take ownership of my part in its unraveling.

Before he tried to kill me, we were two people who could not make it work. After his hands wrapped around my neck – that belonged to him alone.

The sun is slowly disappearing behind the trees in our backyard and I close my eyes, leaning back in my chair.

I see that nineteen year old girl floating around the room in the most incredible wedding dress I had ever seen. There were rhinestones and pearls. Reams of endless satin and lace. It fit her as if it was made for her.

There is a swoosh sound with each simple movement of her fit body. Her face is clear of any wrinkles and her eyes, shining.

She moves through the room with a quiet confidence as she visits with each guest sitting at dinner tables arranged around the dance floor. She stops briefly, checks her reflection in the mirror of the large windows facing the lake.

She is unfazed of any potential harm that lies ahead, a few years down the road. Now, nearing fifty, I want to reach back in time.

I want to hold her.

I also want to shake her.

But mostly, I need to forgive her. Forgive her for not knowing.

Forgive her for the rose-colored glasses.

Forgive her for making what would become the worst decision of her life. Because she didn't know.

It is amazing what twenty-five years will do for a person.

I continue to learn every day about people. I watch and I listen. Picking up on the imperfections that live within all of us. Picking up on the things that make people good. Paying attention to the things that make humans behave badly.

None of us come into this world, completely grounded. With eyes wide open and stealth ability to see a villain versus someone with genuine motives.

There are no protections against bad people.

Twenty-five years ago, my eyes were not open.

They were slivers in the night.

When we arrived at our hotel for the night, still dressed in our wedding clothes, strangers in the lobby smiled and congratulated us as we passed.

It felt like a fairy tale—one of those moments you believe will last forever.

My gorgeous gown rustled with every step, my veil drifting gently around my face, and he held my hand, sharp and confident in his black tuxedo. I remember feeling like a woman.

But I was still a teenager.

My brain is not fully formed. My world is not fully explored.

My boundaries are not fully built.

He was already built.

Already formed.

Already certain.

That certainty felt safe at the time.

It was not.

I remember thinking how perfectly everything had fallen into placc, never imagining how fragile that perfection would one day prove to be.

I see myself drifting off to sleep, tucked in under crisp, white hotel sheets. My husband is probably nearby, yet he isn't there, in my memory. Curious, he has vanished from my mind. Frankly, I don't even think we slept together that night.

"I forgive you, my sweet girl," I whisper now.

"You had no idea of knowing how this would end. Nobody did. Time to release your guilt now. It was his choices that left you bloodied..."

Today is just a date on the calendar.

Nothing more.

Nothing less.

It does not mark the beginning of a marriage.

It marks the day a nineteen-year-old girl stepped into a life she could not yet comprehend.

And the day a nearly fifty-year-old woman can finally say: You were young.

He was not.

And that matters.

CHAPTER 12

Who Was She?

I didn't grow up with a mother. I never truly knew who she was.

Everything I know about my mother comes from what has been shared with me over the years. Which to be honest, isn't much.

I fear I will always struggle to come to terms with the terrible truth that she is dead. When I was younger, I didn't yet understand the weight of it—it was simply always there.

"*Your Mamma is dead.*"

A sentence spoken without ceremony, without explanation, and without room for questions at first. Then as I grew, more age appropriate information would be shared with me.

Yet, it wasn't like in the movies, where a child is finally told some life-altering secret.

There was no moment of discovery. This was real life and I simply always knew. I would pass her portrait sitting on top of our tv console and know that was my Mom and that she was no longer alive.

I have no memory of her voice. I never got to experience her warm touch at an age that I would be able to remember. The only time she touched me was when I was an infant so I have no sense of what it felt like to be held by her.

My idea of a mother was pieced together from watching others, from quiet observation, and from imagining what might have been. I mourned something I never actually had.

I still mourn that today.

It's a quiet pain that every once in a while, rises to the surface and I find myself locking myself in the bathroom – standing in the shower with sobs cursing through my body as hot water encompasses me.

The sound of the shower disguising the sounds of my cries.

Of course seeing her name on her gravestone made the absence undeniable.

Proof that she had existed, even if she had never existed *to me.*

I still remember the crackling sound of my shiny black patent leather shoes against the cold, icy snow as I walked with my siblings to bring her candlelight on Christmas Eve.

Each step brings me closer to her; each step tentative as to not slip and fall on the slippery ground.

Down the long cemetery driveway with the black wrought iron gate that appeared as if it came out of a movie set—about three large trees from the end, then left, then five rows over.

Three rows over. Maybe four.

There she was.

Her name glaring back at me, the same name as mine.

Our name.

Hers etched into stone above a body buried far beneath the ground, and mine carried forward without her.

Without her guidance.

Not to touch.

Not to see.

There never was a warm hug waiting for me.

No familiar voice was happy to greet me.

Just a name written in gold on a granite slab, trying to stand in for a life I never got to witness.

Shiny shoes. Crisp white snow.

Tear drops might have gone unnoticed, but none of us kids fooled anyone – least of all, each other. We weren't just grieving her death. We were grieving the relationships we never had. The questions we never got to ask. The love we never got to receive as we were left here on earth to live, breathe, grow, mature, laugh, travel, marry, have children.

Everything a life ought to hold – we've all had to do without her as our witness and our cheerleader.

When I became a mother myself, that absence came with me. I mothered from instinct and intention rather than memory.

I feel that I have mothered my children guided by love, more than anything.

I have gotten it wrong many times over the years, not making the best of decisions, yet I am keenly aware that I too was in need of growing up. I may have grown alongside my children, trying to figure things out as I went along.

I have always been determined they would never have to imagine what a mother's love felt like.

I never want my kids to question my love for them. They are my breath, my soul, my morning light and all the stars in the sky.

Still, there were moments I wished I could ask her how to do this – how to be steady, how to be enough – only to remember she wasn't there to ask.

The ache never fully leaves.

It just changes shape.

It becomes quieter, more familiar.

It shows up year after year.

Hence the candlelight on Christmas Eve.

Fresh flowers in springtime.

Orange blooms in the fall.

A wreath during winter.

And still, the question lingers – soft, unanswered, and forever.

Who was she?

CHAPTER 13

American Cars, Crawdads And Dolly

When I was little, my favorite place in the world was the passenger seat of my father's car.

To me, it was magnificent – a large maroon American car with velvet-soft seats the same deep shade of red. It felt luxurious in a way I didn't yet have words for.

Whenever we drove, country music filled the car. Whether it came from the radio or a cassette tape, I don't remember.

I only remember Dolly Parton, Kenny Rogers, Tammy Wynette, and Patsy Cline pouring through the speakers as we wound through the narrow roads of my homeland, Norway.

I knew every word to Dolly's songs.

Jolene.

9 to 5.

Coat of Many Colors.

Tennessee Mountain Home.

I sang them loudly sitting next to my smiling dad. In that passenger seat, it felt like nothing bad could touch me. It was just the two of us and the road ahead.

If I were to guess, I first learned English around six or seven years old. We had vacationed in California a couple of times by then, so the timeline fits. I didn't know it then, but I was practicing for a life far away from Norway, singing those words phonetically before I understood them.

That said, Dolly was my idol!

She was beautiful!

She seemed kind, yet quirky and sweet. Knowing now what I didn't know then, she was a brand. Embellished hair, clothes, make-up. It was genius and still is today. Maybe that is how America first slipped into my life – not through an airport, but through Dolly's voice drifting across the dashboard.

I would look forward to little road trips with my dad and one stands out more than others.

With Dolly coming through the speakers, we made our way up into the mountains. I still remember today, how the air outside was cold coming in through the small opening in the car window.

In the trunk were white styrofoam containers.

Empty.

"Where are we going Pappa?" I had asked.

"You'll see. It's a surprise." he answered with a smile.

Before long, we arrived. And soon the two styrofoam containers would be filled to the brim with crawdads.

Live crawdads.

I had never seen anything like it.

"You'll like them," Pappa said.

"I will boil them and then I'll show you how to eat them."

I looked at him, unsure about this, but willing to give it a try.

Once home, Dolly's music now forgotten, my father dumped both containers of the slippery little creatures into our downstairs bathtub. Filling it up a little with cold water, he asked me to keep an eye on them while he started water in a pot on the stove.

I remember picking several up, literally having a little dive contest from the edge of the tub with these mini lobsters. Soon my dad came with a bucket and left with a load to boil. Soon they were piled high, no longer black, but a sharp red in color.

I hesitated before taking my first bite, watching my father twist the tail like it was second nature.

We all ate and enjoyed that evening. Saturdays were usually reserved for special dinners and this was definitely something else.

Now fast forward a little. My father has died and I have moved away from the narrow roads in the mountains of Norway.

I brought Dolly with me, often streaming from the radio or my cassette player, once I made a new home in America. At sixteen, this is where I would make my new home.

Sometimes when I hear those old songs now, I am right back in that maroon car, the mountains rising around us.

Soon an amazing opportunity presented itself and I knew I had to go. Dolly would be at a bookstore near me! I had to meet her.

After about two hours, or was it three, the last three numbers were called into her private signing room. There was a person in front of me and I lingered back, giving them space.

But, there she was.

The Dolly from my childhood, riding in my late father's American car, with her voice filling the air.

"She's absolutely beautiful!" I thought to myself as I got closer.

And, after handing her a book to sing, I said as much. She thanked me while scribbling her name down inside the cover.

"I sang your song 'Coat of Many Colors' when I was ten years old in school in Norway" I burst out. She stopped and looked up. With only a smile Dolly owns, she looked me straight in the eyes.

"Oh, I can see that. You are definitely Scandinavian with those beautiful blue eyes and your blonde hair."

I was in heaven! And, I silently thanked my dad for introducing me to country music growing up.

Country music and live crawdads.

What a combination huh?

I thanked Dolly, said something else and she said something back. What I can't tell you.

It was just too much. I was floating on air having actually met Dolly freaking Parton and it felt like a dream.

After leaving, I sat in my car briefly before making my way out of the parking lot.

Then I saw it.

A limo pulling out from my left waiting to exit the parking lot as well.

Instinctively I honked my horn and stuck my left hand out the driver side window and waved.

I held my breath. Would she wave back?

Dolly didn't disappoint. Soon a slim hand popped out from the rear right window and waved back at me.

I realized then that some people we lose never really leave. My father was right there in the passenger seat beside me. Our places in the car had shifted, but there was no doubt he was there with me.

As I drove, I wanted so badly to call my father. He would have been floored.

"What, you met Dolly freakin' Parton?" he would have hollered through the line. I could hear his laugh.

Then it was over. The limo pulled into traffic and so did I. I had to get home to prepare for a wedding I was photographing that afternoon. Life moving forward, as it does.

Some people inherit money or land. I also inherited country music and courage.

"Yes, pappa, I sure did. Thank you for American cars, Dolly and crawdads. I miss you."

CHAPTER 14

May 7th, 1985

It was a Tuesday, and it began like any other day.

I was twelve years old.

When I opened my eyes, I felt briefly disoriented, forgetting for a moment that I had spent the night at my sister's house.

The confusion passed quickly, replaced by something else entirely. I felt awful. There was a deep, unusual pain in my stomach – twisting, sharp jabs radiating from somewhere inside me.

My body felt wrong.

Because of it, I asked my sister if I could stay home from school. Of course, neither of us could have known what was about to happen.

I stayed in my pajamas and spent most of the morning lying around, interrupted by trips to the bathroom.

Looking back now, I wonder if our bodies know more than we give them credit for. Maybe they sense what our minds can't yet understand or know. Maybe our physical self recognizes that something is about to happen in your life that is unexpected. Our bodies short-circuit in response, urging us to slow down, to stay still, to remain where we are.

It was a little before noon.

I can't tell you if Spring was coming, if the sun was shining or the sky was a calming blue. I can't tell you if it was cold outside or if the sun was making it difficult to see as you drove down the highway.

The sky could have been a dull shade of gray, as if to tell me today would not be a good day. I was a child. Impressions fade over time while other memories are as clear as if it happened last week.

I was walking down the hallway, just past the kitchen, when my sister’s phone rang. Soon, this day would no longer be just a day I stayed home from school with a stomach ache.

My sister picked up the phone.

Then I heard her scream.

“No!” she shouted – in Norwegian.

If you were to ask my sister, however, she did not yell. She remembers things very differently than I do.

Memory is strange and two things can exist at once.

I didn’t know what had happened.

I only knew something was terribly wrong.

That weekend, I went to Oslo with my sister and her fiancee. We had come back late Sunday and although my sister had called our father, she had been unable to reach him. She had driven me by the house on Monday before school. I ran inside, up the stairs, down the hall to my bedroom and grabbed my leather pink backpack.

The door to my father’s bedroom was closed. Or was it open just a little?

Or was it all the way open? I will never know.

It's a detail that seems insignificant yet one I wish I could put into focus.

I raced down the stairs to the waiting car and my sister drove me to school.

Now here is where my memory fractures.

For years I believed my sister picked me up from school that Monday. But as I sit here writing this, I realize I walked home.

I have been told I called her. She told me to just wait outside. That she would come get me. Apparently, I was sitting on our front steps when she arrived.

How does a detail like that disappear for decades?

Grief rearranges things. Trauma edits.

I am perplexed as I write this. In all the years since this day, I seem to have forgotten a very crucial detail leading up to discovering my father had died.

It made sense I would walk home like every other day. It's where I lived with my father after all.

My things were there.

The Dolly Parton cassette tapes.

The Michael Jackson poster on my bedroom door. My favorite stuffed animals. My comfy chair by the window which sadly gave refuge to my clothes when I wasn't wearing them.

My diaries. My bed with the flower bedspread I had inherited from my sister. My favorite pillow. My sketches.

Later she would run into my oldest brother in town and ask him to go by the house to check on our father.

He was now on the other end of that phone, this Tuesday around lunch time.

After my sister hung up the phone, she immediately grabbed her purse and left for our childhood home.

There wasn't much of an explanation at that moment, just that she had to go.

Later I would be told that our oldest brother had found our father, in bed, cold to the touch, no longer breathing, obviously dead, slumped in a pile of his own vomit.

The man who had sat with me many nights as a young child on his lap, had left me. Left us.

There would never be the reassurances he would offer me after I had woken from a nightmare. I would never hear his voice again. No more stories about how he and my mom's romance had begun. No more hugs or goodnight kisses. I would never wake on a Saturday morning to the aroma of bacon and eggs spilling out from our kitchen.

I sat in a heap of arms wrapped around my bent legs on my sister's sofa, rocking back and forth for the next hour. Perhaps it was two.

"Please don't let my daddy be dead...please don't let my daddy be dead..." I prayed over and over in my head.

Many of us idolize the dead. It feels wrong to speak ill of them.

I was aware of his perfect imperfections and I didn't care. His love for his baby daughter was always very present for me.

Not once did I grow up feeling that my father didn't love me.

I did, however, grow up always sensing a bitter sadness that lived within him.

On the outside, he was always happy and funny. That said, he was also strict. But, he loved to joke around. He was often the loudest voice in the room. But, even from an early age, I knew his pain from losing his wife at such a young age to cancer.

After a while, my soon to be brother-in-law had me put my shoes on and grab a jacket.

We were going for a walk, he informed me.

We walked the familiar streets of my home town, slowly making our way towards my father's house. My house.

At the little mini mart near my childhood home, my sister's fiancée made a call. It was 1985 and there were no cell phones.

I begged to go to the house but all the grown ups in my life said no. There was nothing to see.

My sister's future husband finally told me that yes, my father had died in his sleep. It didn't come as a shock.

I couldn't feel him anymore.

Even at twelve, that made sense to me.

I didn't have the language to put words to how I was feeling. That would come much later.

As my feet kept moving that afternoon, back to my sister's apartment, my heart felt numb. I didn't care about the slight breeze cooling my face or the sounds of birds chirping in a stranger's yard as we walked past.

I remember just staring down at my feet and the immediate ground in front of me, forcing my legs to move. I remember thinking of my father, playing the movie reel of my twelve years with him.

I didn't even get to say goodbye.

If there had been an illness, I could have prepared myself, even at twelve years old.

I envision holding his hand, as an old man, me as a grown woman, saying goodbye. That final moment where we would both understand what was happening and make peace with death, on our terms.

A final conversation.

Not this.

Not him dying alone, at forty-seven, in his bed with nobody around.

It felt so incredibly unfair.

It felt cruel.

The cruelty of never being able to ask more questions. Never knowing more. They say that the loss of a loved one gets easier with time.

The loss of my father never truly got easier. It simply shifted its form over the years.

In those early moments, the grief was palpable.

I couldn't feel my own skin. It was almost an out of body experience.

It was as if I was witnessing someone else moving through the world, wounded, afraid, sad and misunderstood. A part of everything I had known to be my life, had left this world so abruptly. There had been no obvious warning signs I would find myself an orphan at twelve years old.

Within a day or two, we all gathered at my father's house. I remember sitting in the living room, knees bent on the carpet, while my siblings occupied other spaces in the room.

The living room was full of light.

My world was not.

I remember the horrible green flower drapes that lined each window and glass door leading to a small side terrace.

There was a chunky, ornate, dark stained wood bar, complete with bar stools and any liquor you could ever want lining the many shelves on the back wall unit.

My father's pipes hung on a round wood and metal contraption by the large window next to what used to be his favorite chair.

A package of loose tobacco nearby. Probably a few ashtrays too. It was the 80's.

To me there was such disbelief that our father had died so suddenly.

In later years, I've been told he had not been feeling well for quite some time. Meaning, my sister and two brothers, probably were more aware of our father's health than their twelve year old little sister.

I knew he wasn't taking care of himself yet in my naïve and rather ignorant mind, he surely wasn't drinking himself to death.

Sadly, this would later be shown to be the cause of my father's death. His liver had burst during the night. Cirrhosis of the liver was evident according to the autopsy.

Although I can't with the utmost certainty say there was an autopsy. There must have been, right? Later I heard something about an aneurysm I think.

Does it matter?

No.

He is still dead.

In the next several weeks and then eventually months and years, I held my father close. I would visit his grave as I had visited that same grave when it was only my mother who had occupied that space.

Now, they have returned to one another.

There is comfort in that.

My mother's death didn't change me, simply for the fact, I never knew her. My father's death, however, did change me.

Over the years, I've fought the tears, the anger, the emptiness of his vacancy. His absence hurt me deeply, in ways that other people don't quite understand.

We had an understanding, my father and I.

He would allow me glimpses of the sadness he felt. He would share with me about my mother. Now, I have lost them both. There would be no more stories only he could tell.

Today I understand there was a lot more to my father.

There are parts of my father's life I don't know about. There are parts of WHO my father was, I also don't know.

Because I was a child.

A child who desperately just loves her father for who he is while in front of her.

And, that is going to have to be ok.

Perhaps some day, I can dive further into who this man was.

Today is not that day.

It may never be the right time.

That too, will have to be ok.

I've come to a place now, where it doesn't feel as heavy as it did then.

My grief occasionally surfaces, but I don't reside in the heartache anymore. Because my father wouldn't want that for me. He will always be my father. Living or dead.

And, I will forever be his daughter, his little girl.

Someone said to me recently, "You had a bumpy start."

Yes.

Yes, I did.

That Tuesday defined me for a long time.

It no longer holds any power.

It is simply a memory of finding out my father died.

What his death gave me - strangely - was endurance.

The day my father died, I learned something without having language for it; You can feel like your insides have collapsed and still keep walking.

That afternoon, I did not stop walking. And I haven't since.

His death gave me strength.

An instinctive desire to keep fighting.

That day — with all its nuances, gaps, and fractured facts — gave me a fierceness that has guided me.

I know my Pappa (dad) is keeping watch. And, there is comfort in that. Grief will forever change over time.

It evolves.

Some days, grief yells loudly.

Some days, grief is on a trip visiting someone else.

Some days, grief walks beside you, urging you forward regardless.

That Tuesday broke something open in me.

It also built something fierce.

CHAPTER 15

If I Can't Have You, Nobody Can

All the while the crudeness of his words kept swirling around in my head, I kept fighting.

"You're going to die today," he had said.

His voice was calm.

Surprisingly.

Factual.

Cruel.

There was no time to freeze or question what was happening. It was glaring me in the face. No room for confusion.

His words made it true.

For a brief moment, I got away from his raging hands.

I crawled on my hands and knees and reached the edge of the nightstand. The phone loomed big on top, just out of reach.

I got a hold of the cord. Yanked hard. The hunter-green phone lurched free and landed awkwardly in my hands.

With trembling hands, I frantically dialed 911 and prayed for the world to stand still. For him to freeze in time. Just long enough for help to answer on the other end of the line.

"Please God! Please…"

There was no answer.

Just a busy signal.

911 was busy.

There would not be anyone coming to help me.

I slammed the receiver down, picked it up again and redialed.

"This cannot be happening…" plays over and over in my mind. *"What exactly is happening?"*

His hands are all over my body. The phone drops to the floor as he hits it out of my hands. The call does not connect.

I try to stand. So does he.

He reaches for my throat, grabbing my arm as I turn to get out of the bedroom. He pulls, holds, scratches every inch of my body he makes contact with.

He is the big bad monster in the room.

Larger than life.

Larger than human.

"Where did this come from?" my mind briefly wonders.

"Where did this violence come from?"

I couldn't help but think back to last week.

He had been so angry when he had stopped by the house to pack up some of his tools and equipment. I had wanted to discuss the divorce and he became unhinged.

Suddenly a small handgun appeared in his hands. He said if I was leaving him, he just wanted to die. He had cried and begged for me to stay.

"I can't do that," I had said.

Somehow I diffused the situation that night. I called his bluff by threatening my own life.

He ran from the house and I cornered him out on the sidewalk. With some coaxing, he had eventually handed over the gun. He had fallen asleep on the sofa and I left.

I tried to sleep in my car in front of a friend's house. I went in when the kitchen lights came on; I hadn't slept a wink.

As I explained the situation to my friends, I made a decision. It was time to cut all financial ties he could possibly gain access to.

It had turned into a day of driving all over to various offices. I removed him from all of my bank accounts, business and personal. Then I closed my photography business, which had both of our names and reopened it in my maiden name.

Later that day, I had to recover my camera equipment. He had stolen it and taken it to his parent's house. I went and got it back – of course I had clients lined up the following week.

Perhaps I should have known, things wouldn't end there.

This had been a pause.

How we ended up here remains a mystery at this moment though.

As I try to reach the front door, there isn't time to think rationally. Or clearly. No time to reminisce about last week's conflict.

Not once did I think he was capable of this sort of violence.

But here we were, in the house we had shared for six years.

"If I can't have you, nobody can!"

His voice brings me back to now.

His face is five inches from mine and his hands are wrapped coldly around my throat.

Pushing tighter and tighter.

I fight him off and make it into the hallway.

I need to find my cell phone.

Those days, these pocket computers we are all familiar with today are somewhere lying around. Rarely within reach. Maybe in a purse. In the car console.

"Get out the front door," I pray.

"Find the front door..."

"If I can't have you, nobody can!"

The echo of his words lingers in the hallway.

He pulls me into our bathroom and before I know what is happening, he grabs my hair, and beats my face against the toilet bowl.

My head explodes.

Chips off a couple of teeth, flew out of my mouth.
Together we fall into the shower, pulling the curtain down with us.

He gets back up ahead of me and sprays my eyes with my deodorant. Then he yanks the towel rack off the wall and presses it against my throat. From behind, he pulls back on the wooden rod.

And it is at that moment I see him out in our back yard.

He is going insane, barking, running back and forth against his dog run lead. He sees me too and we lock eyes.

It is brief, but the confusion is apparent in his behavior.

I break eye contact and focus on getting out of the bathroom.

Pushing my body away from my husband, I make it out and into our kitchen. This is where he corners me.

"I can't go through another divorce."

"If I can't have you, I will kill myself."

Those were his empty threats a week ago.

Now, he was upping the game, although this was no game.

"You have ruined my life and I'm going to ruin yours"

His voice sounds controlled and determined. Cruelty lingers at the edges and then jumps right in with what he says next.

"You are going to die like your folks…you are going to die…"

A large salad bowl comes crashing down on my head. I hesitate. I sway but I keep my balance.

And then I spotted it.

A small steak knife resting innocently in the drying rack on the counter.

Before I know what I was doing, I grab it and twist around to face him. It is as if I leave my body, viewing myself from above.

I see myself stab him in the left side of his neck.

His face registers shock and outrage.

Quickly he simply yanks the knife out, yelling as he chases me towards the door. I hear the knife hit the floor as my hand reaches the door knob.

"I'm dying" he dramatically yells.

I make it to the front door only seconds before he catches up to me. I try to open the door but my left hand becomes trapped between the door and the frame.

I pull the door while he pushes.

I am desperate to open it and run.

He is desperate to keep me prisoner.

For a second, he cracks the door open just enough to gain momentum – then he slams it shut on my hand.

Pain rips through me.

I scream, a sound I don't recognize as my own. My words are incoherent.

I tear my hand free and hold it to my chest as if soothing a crying baby. It feels as if it's on fire. Stabbing agony shots through my knuckles and up my arm, leaving me gasping for air.

I am shaking violently while rocking my body for some kind of comfort. I try to just take a breath.

I am not trying to escape anymore.

I am trying to survive.

CHAPTER 16

The Sand Beneath My Feet

When I was a young girl growing up in a small town in Norway, I escaped to the beach whenever I could. I would hop on my bike and race down the hills from my neighborhood in search of the sand.

I rode past friends' houses, through narrow streets, taking shortcuts to reach the other side of town for that breathtaking view. For the kind of space that surrounds you and quietly slows you down.

Even on dreary, cloud-covered days something called out to me, pulling me toward the waves and salt-heavy sea air.

I would park my bike and climb down toward the sand and scattered rocks.

Inside my backpack there was a journal, a sketch pad, and a handful of pencils and pens.

Most days there was no one else in sight.

The place felt created just for me.

As I lowered myself onto a familiar spot near a rock wall, I exhaled and let my eyes wander across the open water stretching endlessly before me.

I never knew exactly what I was searching for. Only that comfort lived there somewhere.

In that vast landscape, I felt small in a way that soothed me. The world was large, steady, and unconcerned with my pain. In the white caps crashing along the shoreline, I saw love.

I saw hope.

As I sat there, the air light against my skin, my gaze drifted to where the ocean and sky blurred into one endless horizon. My lungs filled slowly, and when I exhaled, my entire body softened in a way I still struggle to explain.

After my father died, there was so much sadness. The beach became my refuge.

I missed him with an ache that hollowed me out.

Knowing he would never stand in front of me again gutted me.

He was bigger than the sea. Larger than the waves.

He was imperfect, I know now, but he was always my dad.

As a child, I searched for peace at that shoreline, though I didn't yet understand what it would come to mean in my life.

I loved the ocean then.

I love it today, living in what feels like another lifetime.

The beach steadies me, holds me for a moment and gives me permission to breathe. It gives me pause – the steady rhythm of the waves, the promise of returning over and over to shore.

Then I jump back on my bike and navigate familiar roads back home.

Ready to face whatever chaos comes next.

CHAPTER 17

Trying To Make Responsible Decisions

The man in front of me wore a sharp, light gray suit. His fingers moved effortlessly across the keyboard, entering the information I had just given him.

I had attempted to dress business-like too, after all, this was a business transaction. Black slacks — the same ones I wore to photograph weddings — a white blouse, and a black jacket. I felt grown up doing this grown-up thing.

I was excited. Nervous, but excited.

As I fumbled with my wallet and checked my account register, I peeked over at him. He was good-looking, probably in his forties, clean-cut hair, focused eyes. He wasn't smiling, but he wasn't scowling either. Looking back now, he was simply doing his job — unaware of how monumental this moment felt to me.

To him, it was routine.

To me, it was a turning point.

Today was the day I would take charge of my money.

The inheritance I received when I turned eighteen was slipping away, drained quickly by a man who loved to spend it. And I let him.

Somewhere along the way, it stopped being mine.

It became ours before I even realized what was happening.

At first, it was subtle.

A bill here.

Camera equipment there.

Then the wedding.

Vehicles. Old engines. Tools.

More things than anyone could track.

I started to fear it would all disappear.

So today, the man in the gray suit — a bank employee — was helping me secure a portion of it. Thirty thousand dollars into an eighteen-month CD. Higher interest. Untouchable.

And more importantly – he wouldn't be able to touch it.

It was a big step.

A necessary one.

Still, a quiet fear lingered. Not that my husband would physically hurt me – but that he would be furious that I had done this without him.

I argued with myself the entire time.

"It's my money," I kept repeating in my head.

"I can do what I want with my money."

After signing the documents and completing the transfer, I walked out holding a thin packet of papers — proof that I had done something right.

Something responsible. I felt light and uneasy all at once as I drove home.

The house was empty when I arrived. I settled into my office to work while I waited for him to get home.

A couple of hours passed.

When he walked through the door, I told him what I had done.

I explained my fear — how quickly the money was disappearing, how this felt like the smart thing to do. For us. For the future. I was proud of myself. I could hear it in my voice. Then he spoke.

His face darkened as he leaned toward me.

"You can't do this. What if we need that money now?" he snapped.

"I can't believe you. This is the stupidest thing you've ever done. You're going to call them right now and tell them you changed your mind."

He kept talking, louder and angrier, but I stopped listening.

He grabbed the kitchen phone from the wall and shoved it into my face.

My resolve dissolved.

I dialed the bank.

After a few moments, I heard the same man's voice from earlier that day. I told him something had come up. That it wasn't a good time. Maybe down the road. Reluctantly, he said it wouldn't be a problem. He'd cancel the transfer.

When I hung up, I didn't know how to feel. I told myself he was probably right. We might need that money. Locking it away was a stupid idea. He's right, I thought.

Years later, I would recognize it for what it really was.

Control.

I had no backbone to defend what I knew was right.

He had me running in circles, convincing me I wasn't capable of making big choices – not with money.

Not with my life.

CHAPTER 18

Who Decides?

Who decides who lives and who dies?

I've asked myself that question for as long as I can remember.

Since I was a little girl, crying at night, whispering prayers to a God I hated because he took my mother away.

What kind of God takes a thirty-two-year-old woman from her four children and her husband?

What could she have possibly done to deserve that kind of ending?

I used to cry myself to sleep wondering who she even was. I knew her name. I knew her face from photographs.

But photographs don't tell you how someone laughed.

Did she like chocolate?

They don't tell you what she smelled like.

Or if she sang in the kitchen when no one was listening. She was mine, and she wasn't, all at the same time.

And now, more than fifty years later, I still cry sometimes. Usually when it's quiet and dark and my brain won't shut up…

Still wondering if she ever thought about leaving us before she did, even though she didn't choose for cancer to take her.

So, who decides?

Is it God? Is it chance?

Is it just life being life and not caring who gets hurt in the process?

Because I cannot wrap my head around believing in a God who stands back and watches the cruelty that people inflict on each other every single day.

The judgments. The hatred.

The casual way people disappear from their children's lives, either by choice or by coffin.

Leaving a little girl sitting in front of a tombstone, crying so hard she can't breathe. The name staring back at her is her mother's name. Yet, it is also her name.

It's carved into cold stone and she can't understand why her chest feels like it is being split open from the inside.

She can't understand why this hurts so fucking much. So much that she is wanting to dig into the dirt just to see if death looks different underground. Just to understand it. Just to prove it is real.

Morbid, right?

That same little girl grows up and becomes a mother herself. Completely unprepared. Pretending she knows what she is doing while quietly hoping her children never notice she is guessing most of the time.

Why did I get to live?

I wasn't even supposed to, not really.

At birth, I didn't have great odds. Born about two months early. But here I am.

Breathing. Aging. Making mistakes. Loving people. Losing people.

So, who made that call? Who looked at my mother and me and decided she goes and I stay?

Maybe it's survivor's guilt. Actually, it is the survivor's guilt.

I have carried it like a second heartbeat my entire life.

I lived and she didn't.

And I hate that sentence even as I write it.

Because if she had lived, my children wouldn't exist.

The people who are my entire universe would simply not be here. That thought alone stops me from being angry for too long.

Gratitude and grief tangled together. It's impossible to separate them.

I think about my children constantly. About whether they see me clearly or just through the lens of my failures.

The years I drank too much. The times I was louder than necessary. Too blunt. Too friendly. The moments I embarrassed them by speaking before thinking, by loving too openly, too clumsily, too much.

I hope someday they understand that I have always led with love. Even when I was doing it badly.

Even when I was doing it drunk.

Even when I was doing it broken.

Every day I wake up and wonder what exactly I am supposed to be doing with this life I somehow kept.

Am I happy? Yes. I think I am. But there is always that word sitting quietly beside happiness like it's waiting for its turn.

But.

There has to be more than surviving.

I have survived pain.

I have survived people dying.

People leaving.

I survived my husband trying to murder me. So now what? What do you do after you realize you are still here when you weren't entirely sure you would be?

Some days I convince myself this writing is pointless. That I am not an author.

Not even an aspiring one.

That these words will sit quietly somewhere and never be read by anyone who didn't already love me out of obligation or blood.

And still, I write.

Because I want to leave something behind that says I was here.

That all those mornings I got out of bed when I didn't want to mean something.

That keeping a roof over our heads and food on the table and safety inside our walls mattered.

That the messy, imperfect, loud, stubborn love I gave my children counts for something even if it wasn't graceful.

Sometimes I stop and try to imagine the day when I am what my parents are to me now – a memory. Just stories and photographs and maybe a few personality traits that get passed down like eye color or sarcasm.

The world spinning forward without me noticing.

That thought terrifies me in a way. I don't talk about it out loud very often. Because I know I am not more special than anyone else walking around breathing right now. And knowing that makes death feel both ordinary and horrifying at the same time.

I am still that little girl who met death too early. I knew it before I knew how to speak English. I felt it before I understood permanence. I saw it before I understood time.

And even now, after decades of standing in its shadow, it still scares me. Familiar does not mean comfortable. It just means you recognize the shape of the thing that frightens you.

I want to believe there is a reason buried somewhere inside the chaos. I don't know if I actually believe that, but I want to. With my whole heart.

I will probably spend the rest of my life turning it over and over like a penny in my pocket, feeling its edges, looking for an answer that may not exist. I suspect I am not the only one asking these questions. I suppose there is comfort in knowing that I am not speculating alone.

Maybe nothing is ordered the way we pretend it is.

Maybe life is just a string of moments tied together loosely, some knots tighter than others.

Maybe some things are fate.

Maybe some things are predestined.

Maybe most things just happen because they do, and we build meaning afterward because living without meaning feels unbearable.

People wake up one morning and the next morning belongs to someone else.

I read once about living the dash.

That small line carved into stone between the day you arrive and the day you leave. Such a tiny mark to hold an entire life.

We rarely see the beginning coming.

We almost never see the ending. All we really have is the space in between.

So live the dash.

Live in between.

That is the hope that fuels me forward.

And makes me get up every day to see the sunrise.

CHAPTER 19

Just Because I'm Your Wife

There's a shift in the air. At first it is subtle, but it is unmistakable.

Younger me feels excited because you believe this is what intimacy looks like and what marriage is supposed to hold. You tell yourself the anticipation and the intensity must be part of the sexual thrill and is part of belonging to someone completely.

In the beginning, maybe it was fine. I assumed it was.

I honestly don't remember our sex life. Only small glimpses.

That absence feels telling now. My mind did what it had to do to protect me – it sealed those moments away, blurred them into nothing.

It should have been desire and bliss, but I fear it was confusion, dread and compliance.

A much older self now understands that excitement born from obligation isn't excitement at all.

It's conditioning.

It's learning to read someone else's moods for survival and mistaking his behavior for intimacy. I didn't know how to separate my own wants from his expectations, so I folded them together and called it marriage.

Complete bullshit.

I figured this was how it was supposed to be. And I was wrong.

To remember any of this, I had to dig — into old journals, into handwriting that belonged to a younger version of me, into words written without knowing they would one day matter.

Although there isn't much detail, there's enough there that tells me everything I need to know. Those pages speak of him when I could not. They hold truths I wasn't ready to name then, moments I minimized, softened and misunderstood.

I see the pattern clearly with how elusive I was in my descriptions of spending the day in bed together.

I don't speak about how he touched me this way or that way. I don't speak about how he made me feel sexy, loved and attractive. I say none of those things, because those things were not happening to me while we were intimate.

I remember on numerous occasions, he would glare at my thin body and vomit words about how if I lost a few pounds, I could totally be a playboy bunny.

What I once believed was passion was something else. Maybe it was fear dressed up as devotion.

There must be a reason I have such limited memories of it. We were together for almost six years.

I had to fake it to get him to climax on my stomach so it would be over. That I do in fact remember. And me, wondering what the fuss regarding sex was all about.

I frankly do not remember much more. I view that as a gift.

I do remember his long hair hitting my face as he kept pushing his penis inside me. I hated how his hair smacked my face and recoil at the memory even now.

Never mind, he didn't trust that I was taking the pill, so he would pull his penis out, grab it and choke it off, spraying it on my stomach.

I was his wife and he knew I wanted children more than anything, yet he could never allow me to become pregnant.

He would just let me rescue more cats and eventually a dog.

But a baby?

Hell no.

I should only love him. Because he was so amazing and did so many amazing things to further our future.

Most definitely not. Wrong on so many levels.

I am sitting here writing this and I still can't figure out his ultimate end game. How long did he figure I would stay without starting a family? Did he think I would just abandon the idea altogether years down the road?

It goes beyond saying, I am thankful we did not have children together.

Although he never said as much out loud–that he did not want children – I am grateful every day that I never carried his. His bloodline did not continue through me and at the end of the day, there was nothing to tie us together as the years went on.

The first time my husband raped me, was on our living room floor. The television was on, but there was a porn tape running off the VCR. He started it off with being sweet.

Wanting to spice it up.

He even put a pillow under my head before he straddled me.

Before he pulled my panties off.

Before he moved my bra just so, he could abuse my nipples. It began just fine. Until it wasn't fine anymore.

The ceiling became the walls and walls became the ceiling. The coffee table next to the disgusting sofa loomed to my right. He wasn't looking at me at all.

I became a vessel for his dick.

Was I even in the room anymore?

I felt myself looming above, watching. And I wanted to throw up.

I glanced up to my left, to the television screen, seeing a man fucking some woman who was also playing a part.

When I turned my eyes back to this man I was married to, he had no eyes for me.

They were glued to the television and whatever party was happening on-screen. I may as well have been a blow up doll.

The only difference was I had a pulse.

I had never in my life felt so unloved.

Yet I sighed and moved my hips just enough to make it stop. It worked and he pulled his cock out just in time to spray it all over my stomach.

Good for him.

I was such a good wife, wasn't I?

I couldn't help it and started to cry ever so silent. I turned my face away from the screen of the television so he wouldn't see. Not that he was paying any attention to me at all.

My husband had just raped me while thinking he was spicing things up.

The next time he raped me was while on a trip to Alaska.

I was hired to shoot a wedding and we chose to make it a vacation by extending our stay for about four days. Work the wedding, see some sights and try to build what was broken.

Upon arriving in Alaska, we saw the sights, met with the clients and I photographed the wedding I had been hired to shoot.

And then, one morning before I even had a chance to have coffee, he moved over from the left side of the bed, to be right on top of me.

The sheets were bright white, the light was starting to come in from the vast windows in our hotel room.

I felt blindsided.

His skin touched my skin. We kissed. I tried to like it. I tried to engage, but there was nothing. Any spark had simply vanished and I was done.

His touch felt cruel.

His touch was unwanted.

He became aggressive and I asked him to stop. He didn't stop.

He kept kissing my neck and invading my vagina with his fingers, but I was all dried out.

Literally and emotionally.

He proceeded to enter me, so forcefully, I let out a painful cry. He kept going and going and going.

My insides were on fire.

I tried to focus on everything else. I looked past him to the ceiling, to the windows, to the door, wanting to just run.

The door is not that far.

Fifteen feet between myself and freedom.

If only.

I didn't run.

I stayed, motionless eventually, and I let it happen.

At about a buck thirty-five, five feet and ten inches tall, I felt so small. So insignificant.

He was the giant in the room. He had taken everything.

My family relationships, my friends, my sense of self. He did it so on the sly, I didn't even notice.

Put me behind a camera and I would control a room, an event, a Wedding, a Family Portrait Session – put the camera back in its place, I became a nobody.

Now he had taken my body too.

Again.

It was too late to do anything but simply lay there while he finished.

Lay there while he rolled off to my left, leaving one arm coddling my chest, grinning. I took a deep breath and found a spot in the ceiling to focus on.

He never recognized what he had just done. Ignorance is bliss right?

Or was it another attempt at showing his power? I don't remember the rest of the trip.

I'm sure all of my fancy equipment was repackaged and sent back home on various planes. Maybe I should have sent him back alone and stayed.
In the crisp air and beautiful landscape, I could have stayed.
Such a vast land of beauty, that part will always stay with me as a fond memory.

Nothing he did could take Alaska's beauty away.

Alaska didn't make me want to run; he did. Alaska almost made me want to stay. To be anywhere in the world where he wouldn't be.

I don't know what telling this part of my story will do, but it needed a voice. A truth I couldn't keep quiet about any longer.

I don't feel small anymore. I did in that Alaska Hotel room.

I wish I had connected my brain to logic a hell of a lot sooner.

Real relationships should be intimate, loving, open and adventurous with both participants agreeing to what works for them.

Real sexual relationships will never live up to any fantasy that happens in an adult movie because it isn't real.

There is nothing wrong with having fun in the bedroom. Just make sure the fun is consensual.

Monsters wear all sorts of masks.

Sometimes they are the ones we marry.

CHAPTER 20

He's Relentless

He caught up to me just outside the front door, at the bottom of the concrete steps. I was on the ground faster than I could have ever imagined. He is on top of me, forcing my face into the ground, his hands around my neck once more.

I could smell the concrete.

Gasoline, maybe oil—something sharp and industrial. I pretend to pass out hoping that would confuse him.

Just go limp.

Just survive.

At that moment, everything goes dark and I'm no longer present in my own body.

The next thing I know, I am being thrown back into the house. My body clips a rocking chair before I roll onto the floor.

When I manage to focus, I see a man I barely recognize – furious, unhinged – holding a shotgun. It's pointed directly at my body. His finger is clearly on the trigger.

"Oh, fuck. How am I going to get out of this?" I think to myself instantly.

At that moment, I am flooded with everything I haven't done yet. The life I still wanted.

The children I never had but wanted with my whole heart. Who was this man?

Who was the person I married?

The shame and self-blame would come later. For not seeing the red flags. For not knowing.

Nothing makes sense – and yet somehow it all does – at the exact same moment. But there is no room for philosophy when you're staring into the open mouth of a shotgun.

When you can see it moving – slowly – up your legs toward your heart. You know exactly where he's aiming. You know what comes next.

It's as if I hear the boom before it happens.

In a second or two, my mind runs through the future.

The barrel traces my legs, my hips, my stomach, my chest.

I wait.

I wait for the pain. I expect to see blood seeping through my shirt. I wait for the moment when my breathing becomes shallow and then impossible.

I look him square in the eyes.

Mine are burning – tears, confusion, sadness, anger – every shred of hope drained from my body.

I speak to him without saying a word.

There is a silent conversation between us, one he clearly understands.

It feels as if several minutes go by, yet it was probably no more than ten seconds.

"How could you? How the fuck did we get here?"

He offers no comfort.

No answers.

"*Did you already shoot me?*

Am I dead?

Why are my ears ringing?

Why is there a hole in our ceiling?

Why am I holding the shotgun?

And why isn't there a gaping hole in my chest as I was certain I had been shot?"

He doesn't answer.

There is nothing left to say.

CHAPTER 21

Buying And Selling What Exactly?

It's disguised as a day out together – a stop in a well-known city that celebrates my Norwegian heritage. They hold parades there for Norway's Independence Day. It's charming. Touristy. Safe.

He offers the outing nonchalantly as we get ready and head out.

In his truck, he drives. I watch the city pass by mostly in silence. It isn't tense. It isn't joyful. It just…is.

Soon he turns down Main Street and parks near a large building that sells boats and outboard motors.

I feel a flicker of irritation as he opens the door for me before we go inside. By then, I suspect what this outing is really about. The realization nags at me, yet I say nothing.

A salesman – maybe one of the owners – leads us through the building and into the back, where broken down outboard motors sit waiting for repair. My future husband lights up. He knows how to rebuild them from spare parts and sell them through ads in the paper.

He walks through the shop pointing at the ones he wants.

I try to follow along at first, but eventually I hang back, waiting for them to finish. I have no idea how many he is buying, and truthfully, I don't care. This buying and selling venture is his interest, not mine.

I just want to leave as the smell of oil and gasoline settles thickly in my nose. I linger near the front door, ready for us to go.

Suddenly, my future husband and the salesman emerge from the back warehouse. After some discussion and the tapping of keys on a computer, it appears the deal had been finalized between the two men. He waves me toward the counter.

"Hey, write the check, okay?"

As I step closer, I am not sure I heard him correctly. He repeats himself, this time clearly not posing it as a question.

I hesitate, unsure what to do next. Something shifts inside my body, a quiet alarm sounding somewhere deep within me, yet I don't have the awareness to listen to it. I place my purse on the counter, reach inside, and pull out my checkbook.

The man behind the counter prints an invoice and slides it toward me. I lean forward to read it and inhale sharply.

It is over twelve hundred dollars.

Everything in me tells me not to do it, yet it doesn't feel like a choice has been offered.

My future husband has put me in a position that doesn't allow me to refuse without risking embarrassment in front of the salesman. Deep down, I suspect this request has been pre-planned.

Even walking through the shop earlier, looking at those broken down motors, I had braced for it.

He is an expert at making me do things even when I know better — even when I know this was a waste of money. He makes me believe his love comes with conditions.

If I don't give him what he wants, he will surely abandon me.

The pen hovers in my hand for a fraction of a second too long before he nudges me to hurry.

I press the pen to the paper and write the check. As I sign my name in the bottom right corner, I mumble something about him paying me back once he repairs and sells the motors. I vaguely remember him agreeing, though as time would reveal, that repayment would never come.

Throughout the years that followed, this pattern repeats itself. Not once does he return money to my accounts.

Looking back, I am horrified by how easily I allowed it to happen. He held the power of love over me — convincing me that no one could ever love me the way he did.

I believed him.

I believed I was damaged goods because grief had already carved deep wounds in my heart after losing my parents. He framed his devotion as something rare, something better than any other person could give. He told me no one else would understand me the way he did.

He bought flowers often, along with offerings of love in countless Hallmark cards filled with cliché phrases that eventually stopped landing the way they should.

My memory is fragmented about who paid for romantic dinners when we went out. I believe in the beginning he picked up the check. Over time, though, my inheritance quietly began covering most of our meals.

But he loved me.

He was my safe harbor.

At the end of each day, he was there for me. On his days off, he spent his time with me.

He began assisting at my photography gigs so we could spend even more time together. He encouraged me as my business grew, and through his approval, he made me feel worthy. I felt grateful he chose me.

Over time, however, I began to see his desire to spend so much time together – even working weddings beside me – as something else.

Quietly, he was keeping an eye on his prized possession.

Something inside me recognized the unspoken contract forming between us. Writing checks to support his hobby felt less like generosity and more like proof of loyalty. I couldn't risk losing him. He had become the center of my world, and I feared that disagreeing might make him reconsider marrying me altogether.

I was convinced I would never find another man who could understand the emptiness left by my parents' absence or take a chance on a girl broken in ways she couldn't yet recognize.

I wasn't timid or shy around other people.

I was confident when working my craft, capable of orchestrating a wedding from start to finish. I genuinely cared about the people in my photographs, and although I was still refining my work, it was something I deeply loved.

When my boyfriend — and eventually my husband — began working with me, he had the idea that we should wear matching suits, even purchasing our own tuxedos.

I was a woman wearing a tuxedo for a husband who adored my long blonde hair and threw a fit when I cut it short near the end of our marriage.

Yet there I stood in that tuxedo, made to feel like a man.

The suit couldn't hide my curvy hips or my average chest, but in hindsight, I wonder if he simply didn't want anyone to truly see me.

Among crowds of groomsmen and fathers of the bride, I blended in with them rather than standing beside the women in elegant gowns, flawless hair and makeup, towering heels, and effortless confidence.

The outboard motors were picked up later and piled into our backyard, where he worked on them.

Some he managed to repair.

Others ended up abandoned sideways in his small shop — or worse, scattered across the yard. Twelve hundred dollars of mostly useless parts eventually became thousands of dollars' worth of unattractive, rusting *"yard art,"* pelted by rain and snow depending on the season.

It was all funded by a girl who desperately wanted to belong, a girl who felt abandoned after losing her parents so young. He forced himself into the emotional space left vacant from my losses.

He wrapped me in what felt like a soft blanket, and at first, it felt like relief. Grief had left me cold in ways I didn't understand, and his constant presence felt like warmth returning to my body. I mistook the enclosure of the blanket for protection.

Over time, he tucked the blanket tighter and tighter around me.

At first around my shoulders, then around my voice, then around my choices.

In private, I learned to make myself smaller beneath it.

I couldn't risk losing the comfort it offered, so I folded my instincts — my knowing better — into the seams.

I didn't realize the warmth was conditional, that the blanket could be pulled away whenever I refused to write a check or slide over my credit card.

I only knew I was terrified of being cold again, and he understood that fear better than I did.

His comfort slowly became my confinement.

By the time I realized I was suffocating beneath it, I no longer remembered what fresh air felt like.

CHAPTER 22

Making Plans And Setting Goals

About a year earlier, I wrote an entry in my journal while sitting alone in a Coco's restaurant. Reading it now, I feel how much I am holding back.

I choose my words carefully, afraid that if he finds my private thoughts, he will use them against me.

There is almost a secret code woven through the sentences, a language I seem to write only for myself. Although, I'm not sure I was equipped to decipher the code any longer. These thoughts were written such a long time ago.

Still, even through my restraint, I can clearly see the shift beginning. I also remember where I am in my mind during this time and don't need journal entries to remind me of my life.

On the page, I see a young woman starting to change. I am no longer the naïve girl in earlier entries proclaiming her love for her future husband and dreaming of having babies someday.

What stands out just as much is how few journal entries exist between the year we marry and this moment — long stretches of silence where my voice nearly disappears.

So, there I am, in a restaurant alone. I ordered a cup of coffee and a salad after a meeting with a group of remarkable women. I have recently joined their company as a sales consultant for a side gig and am also providing photography work for them.

If I'm honest, finding that group may be saving my life in ways I don't yet understand. Being around them makes me feel capable again – empowered, motivated, and hungry for something more.

For the first time in a long while, I began setting goals.

I share some of those goals with female friends, and they gladly cheer me on. My confidence grows, along with a desire for independence — financial independence, specifically.

We are not being smart with money. He likes to think my inheritance is his to spend as he wants.

The money is not enough to last forever.

Today's version of me would leave it untouched, safely in a bank account back in Norway. But dwelling on what could have been serves no purpose. What matters is that on that evening in Coco's, something inside me was already beginning to wake up.

Interestingly enough, I write:

"I can no longer look to others to achieve any goals and I need to set my own goals and work towards them independently."

I also write about my late father, *"I have to release myself from you in order to survive..."*

I am really talking about my husband, disguising it as a note about my dad. Deep down, I am beginning to understand my need to be free from his emotional and mental manipulation.

Isn't it strange how in this crazy world we live in, we feel the need to disguise our own journal entries out of fear of being "found out" somehow?

I know now that he doesn't have the emotional maturity – even at thirty-nine – to realize that when someone stops loving you, you can't force it.

He wants to insert himself into everything I am doing with my photography business, and it begins to feel like I am being suffocated long before he actually tries to suffocate me for real.

I set goals to pay off debt, buy a home of my own, have children – all things that simply do not appear to be important to him. His words don't reflect that, of course, as he likes to feed me lies.

"When we do this and when that happens, we will have kids," he says.

On that random day in June, I begin making future plans – traveling back home for a visit and advancing within the private sales company I have recently joined.

As far as direct sales goes, it offers real growth, financial opportunity, and tangible rewards for moving up the ladder.

I never intended to abandon my photography. Why should I? What is wrong with wearing many hats? The most successful people try to grow and become better.

Ironically, that question answers itself today.

I do wear many hats now. It has become second nature – to stay busy, to keep building, to continuously improve the life I was given. I almost always have a project underway, dipping my toes into different ventures, learning as I go.

Looking back, I can see it clearly: this isn't restlessness.

It is survival evolving into ambition.

And that said, it is true that even today, almost thirty years later, I still have to land. I am not finished, and many would say I haven't even quite taken flight.

But the leap is coming.

It's coming.

I am starting with this.

Sharing my story and fulfilling a promise I made to myself a long time ago. I've always been a writer, yet for a long time, I couldn't find the right words.

Today, I have at last found my voice.

CHAPTER 23

A Mother's Heartache

Perhaps, in a different universe, a parallel one, but one whereas my mother had lived, the phone rings and it's a stranger from across the pond, telling you that your daughter is okay, but that something terrible has happened.

She calmly asks for more information and as it is given to her, she screams. She starts to cry as more information is shared.

Briefly she covers the receiver and yells at her husband, to pick up the extension.

"He tried to kill her," she screams.

"Honey, pick up the phone!"

Is this the alternative I could have lived? What if I had actually died? What if she had lived?

She would have run upstairs, leaving the receiver off the hook in the office downstairs then racing to grab the one in the hallway upstairs.

She would have wanted the cord to be long enough to reach the bedroom. So she could pack.

With enough information, she finally hangs up.

For a moment, she stands there, at the top of the stairs, in the hallway between the bedrooms her children once occupied.

This wasn't a moment to falter. As my father rushes upstairs, having hung up the office extension, they exchange a look.

No words are necessary. They grab luggage and start filling them with whatever seems needed at that moment.

They have a plane to catch.

My mother is numb. Yet frantic.

And soon anger starts to brew. How dare he?

We trusted you to love and never harm our daughter! It took us ten years to have another child.

She is bewildered as she looks back on the struggle to become pregnant again, after having had three kids in quick concession. Not my baby. You hurt my baby.

And, she just wants to see her youngest daughter. Hold her. Love her and take it all back.

If a bandaid would do the trick, my mother would place them on every inch of my body.

Perhaps make me swallow some, to treat the wounds inside.

My mother would get off that airplane, probably leave her handbag behind, for my father to grab, in her rush to get to me.

Would I be waiting at the gate in this alternate universe?

Or would she and my father have to make their way to the morgue to say their final goodbyes?

I see her and she is racing towards me.

My mother, so simple in her beauty and grace.

She takes my face into her hands, her eyes searching mine, and exhales. For only a few seconds, time stops, and I am home.

Not alone.

Not afraid of the dark.

Knowing exactly where the front door is.

For a moment, my mother is alive, as she wraps her arms around me. So tight, I almost can't breathe.

Her fear is gone because she has her baby in her arms. Her pain is not from losing her child in a violent attack. She can smile again.

Writing this, I want more than anything that my next words wouldn't be what they are. I can't smile at this fantasy of a moment.

Because it never happened.

My mother never loved me this way because she never had the opportunity to. Not that she didn't want to.

My mother is dead.

My parents never boarded a plane for the United States, to comfort their daughter. I never felt her hands cup my face as she searched my eyes for a sign of life.

I never felt her heartache as this diabolical monster had taken something from us all. Our innocence.

My mother didn't have to endure this heartache because she does in fact only live in a picture frame and in the corners of my heart.

But, having the fantasy of this alternate universe somehow brings me just a little bit closer to the woman I never knew.

Just a little.

CHAPTER 24

The Shotgun

It happens fast. The gun is aimed at me, and then I'm no longer on the floor – I'm fighting him for it. I didn't make a choice so much as my body made one for me. Survival took over where my conscious mind could not react in time.

We struggle, our hands trying to get control of the gun. Each of us is trying to get control over the other, but it happens almost on a loop like this day has already been.

Him fighting to kill me and me fighting to live. Over and over again in countless different ways.

I somehow get my finger on the trigger while it's pointed toward the ceiling. I knew it was loaded. I had watched him do it I think but I can't be sure. He could have loaded it before even entering the house earlier that morning. Because who would bring an unloaded weapon to a gun fight?

Is it though, with only one gun?

One gun is enough to do some harm.

Yes, it was most definitely loaded, I think to myself. Doesn't matter when he loaded it. From the time he left his parents' house, armed with a shotgun that didn't belong to him as well as bullets – he had a plan of how he wanted this to end.

I had no real experience with guns, no training, no understanding of all the mechanics – only the certainty that if his finger reached the trigger before mine, I would die.

Looking back now almost thirty years later, I'm struck by how calm that certainty was. It doesn't cause me to panic. Not then and certainly not now. It was just a fact.

Whether I lived or died was balanced in a fraction of a second.

One simple moment stood between me in a casket or me outside that front door, free. All this time later, it does give me pause. Because all the things I would have missed. Then again, I wouldn't have been here to miss it because I would forever be known as the girl who was killed by her estranged husband.

The girl from Norway who came to this land of opportunity to start anew, away from her tragic losses and knowing glances everywhere she went back home.

The shy and naive foreign girl who in Algebra class, almost talked into asking the teacher what the word "cum" meant, but didn't because a kind girl filled her in and probably saved her from detention.

The young woman who showed promise as a photographer and knew when to push the button to capture just the right image.

The blue eyed blonde who needed reassurances that she wasn't too fat.

The woman who came home one day with a fun and funky short hair cut feeling excited about her new do yet found her husband yelling at her telling her *"You look like a boy and you look fucking ugly..."*

I would have been known as the girl who tried and failed.

As I stood in this moment however, trapped in that house, just inside the front door, I barely understood what hinged on one second and on a weapon I never should have been forced to touch.

I kept my finger where it was, not because I knew what I was doing. I absolutely did not know what I was doing. Instinct perhaps. All I knew was that letting go felt impossible.

The sound when it fires is something that never leaves you.

It wasn't just loud – it was violent as if the house itself had been split open. I prayed that someone heard it.

I would continue to hope this the entire rest of the morning.

Turns out, if they did, they didn't come to see what was the matter. The hole itself was small, about the size of a small plum maybe.

There was a surge and a jolt that traveled down my arms. The ringing in my ears looped over and over. The world seemed to tilt. And then stopped all together.

The hole in the ceiling felt unreal, like evidence from someone else's life and not mine. Imaginary smoke hung in the air, dust drifting down. I tried to understand how something so small could create so much destruction.

If that bullet had entered my body, it would have destroyed me. There was no question about that in my mind.

There was never any doubt that I was the one that fired that shot, yet I was questioned about the details of it at length.

As if for a second, the police detectives wondered what my culpability was in all of this.

All I was trying to do was stay alive.

I see it differently now as there is distance between then and now. The facts are clear that yes, I fired that gun but hear me out.

I didn't fire a gun; I interrupted a death.

That hole in the ceiling wasn't just damage – it was proof that I fought back, that my instincts helped me choose to live and act accordingly.

My body and the actions of my body, specifically my hands, chose life for me when my mind could not catch up to the reality of the situation.

Because let me tell you this – looking up at the barrel of a shotgun had never been in my purview.

The cruelest of all wasn't so much having it pointed at me. It was realizing who was aiming it at me.

My husband.

CHAPTER 25

I've Outlived My Father

Grief isn't grief all by itself.

It's love.

If there wasn't love, there would be nothing to miss. And there is no timeline for missing someone. Most people don't understand that. They also don't understand that you can miss someone deeply and still have a beautiful life.

I'm sitting on my back porch – a mishmash of color and comfort. An L-shaped sofa built from pallets years ago, with help from a friend and his tools. It's layered with pillows and outdoor cushions and blankets – the kind of comfort that invites you to stay.

This is where summer afternoons stretch into evenings. Where friendships deepen over food and drink and storytelling. Where there is no judgment, just love. White lights of all sizes hang overhead. A beautiful rug anchors the space beneath a glass coffee table.

Candles – real and faux – flicker inside steel lanterns. If you allow your eyes to wander, you'll quickly discover pots of flowers spilling over at the porch's edge: purple, pink, white, red.

Refusing to be subtle.

An outdoor oasis made to comfort, to calm and bring solitude as well as companionship depending on the day. And sitting here, wrapped in all this light and color, I realize something.

A life can be cracked and complicated and still be beautiful. Still be soft. Still be mine.

Like a chipped coffee mug, it still holds warmth. It still has work to do.

Maybe my so-called terrible life isn't terrible at all. Maybe it's simply one I built – piece by piece – into something worth sitting in.

And tonight, I wish my father was sitting here with me.

In choosing to write this story, I have learned that I just want to be understood. Or maybe I just want attention, some will say. Maybe that is true. Or maybe it's believing that if my story reaches even one person, and they feel less alone, then it mattered.

Maybe it will show how difficult obstacles can be overcome. Smiling again is possible.

Not just a simple smile either but one that transcends.

My heart aches for my father tonight.

The grief is quiet now – not loud, not
sharp – but it lingers. Always.

I have lived a beautiful life alongside
the pain.

I wish with my whole heart that he had lived to meet my son and daughter. My children carry our family in them – in their faces, in their personalities, in their occasional lack of a filter. I know he would have delighted in every nuance.

I can see it so clearly: his laugh, his eyes sparkling, amused and proud of who his grandchildren are becoming.

Of course, these are imagined scenes.

But they feel real enough to ache over.

And perhaps the hardest truth of all.

He died at forty-seven.

By the time this book goes to print, I will be older than forty-seven.

I have outlived my father.

That truth lands differently than I ever imagined it would. It meets me with a strange, heavy tenderness—an awareness that time kept moving even when he could not, and that I am carrying him forward into days he never touched.

As I sit here in this peaceful space, there is both friction and calm. Gratitude and grief.

The knowing that I can't have it both ways. The understanding that I cannot rewrite what was without unraveling what is. If even one moment had unfolded differently, everything that followed would have shifted.

And I might not be sitting here now – on this porch I built, in this life I fought for – surrounded by light.

CHAPTER 26

Resilience Doesn't Always Roar

I don't know how many of you are writers, but lately I find myself questioning everything I thought I knew about myself.

In an effort to understand the girl I was – the one who allowed him to control me the way he did – I've been reading old journals. Pages from what feels like a lifetime ago, some even dating back to when I first moved to the United States from Norway.

I read them now and wonder, "*who was this person?*"

Some days, I'm tempted to throw them all away.

Sixteen-year-old me was painfully naive and shockingly unprepared for the world. She had no real understanding of people or their intentions. If I'm honest, I'm not sure I've fully mastered that even now.

And yet, looking back, it makes total sense. Of course it does.

It is no wonder he was able to hook me. I wanted to be loved so desperately because I believed I wasn't enough on my own. He sensed that, and he fed off it.

I won't give him more credit than he deserves – I wouldn't call him brilliant – but he knew how to play the part.

His attention felt sweet. It felt intentional and safe at first. I should have seen that it wasn't, but I blame that on my sheltered life. Even if it sounds brave to leave your homeland and cross an ocean, I was a sheltered girl. It didn't take much to convince me I was falling in love.

But I know now—I never truly loved him. I didn't even know what love looked like.

What he offered was deceit from the very beginning. And a love built on lies has nowhere to go. It cannot last. It has no foundation.

When something begins with motives instead of truth, collapse is inevitable. Love shouldn't require shrinking.

It shouldn't demand surrendering yourself.

It shouldn't make you feel small.

Real love makes you feel equal. Safe. Free.

I didn't have the language for that then. But somewhere inside, I think I knew.

What I'm learning as I revisit these old pages – marked by my ever-changing handwriting – is that I always had a little fire in my belly, paired with a dash of humor.

I find myself laughing at the random things I chose to write about, at my attempts to be funny simply for the sake of being funny. Even then, I was finding ways to lighten the weight of the world around me.

No one has ever read these entries, and no one probably will. They were never written to be shared. But within them, I see a version of myself who refused to disappear entirely despite his attempts at making me feel small.

Beneath the fear, beneath the confusion, there was wit. There was playfulness. It seems I owned a quiet defiance in choosing humor when life felt heavy.

That side of me still shows up today – a little wiser, maybe softer, but still there. And I'm beginning to believe it wasn't accidental. Maybe humor wasn't just a part of my personality. Maybe it was survival.

A way to stay human. A way to keep going when so much was trying to harden or silence me.

So yes, I believe humor has carried me in countless ways over the past thirty years – and even before.

Resilience doesn't always roar.

Sometimes, it laughs.

CHAPTER 27

Never Give Up

I kept my finger on the trigger after the shot was fired into our ceiling. After pulling it, I simply don't let go. He continues to fight me for it and tries unsuccessfully to load another round into the chamber.

The bullets tumble to the floor and in frustration he yanks it from my hands and throws the weapon off to the side.

Later a detective tells me by keeping the trigger pulled, I had inadvertently prevented more bullets from being loaded.

After he tossed the shotgun aside, he dragged me back into the bathroom. He fought me.

I fought back

I used his body as leverage – jumped, kicked both legs toward the small bathroom window.

The glass shattered.

My ankle screamed when it hit the frame, but adrenaline drowned the pain.

My bare feet landed in shards.

Glass buried itself into my skin.

"I need to get away. Can I fit through that window?"

I wonder with frantic desperation.

I scream out through the opening, praying someone will hear. Vinnie's barks grow louder. I reach without thinking, attempting to pull my body up and out.

Now, my palm is bleeding. More glass embeds into my skin. Yet, I pay no attention to it.

I react to his violence instinctively. I know I must keep going.

A nightmare most often finds us in the middle of the night.

This is daytime.

This isn't a dream and I am not about to wake up.

I am a prisoner in a real nightmare that seems to have no end.

As a child, I had bad dreams constantly. My father would sit beside me, calm me, tell me it wasn't real.

But my father was not here. My mother was not here.

I found myself all alone in a world I no longer recognized.

He had eventually agreed *"living like roommates"* wasn't what he wanted either.

"I understand, this isn't working." he had said last week.

Now I understand nothing.

Everything is happening so fast.

Yet it feels like everything is happening in slow motion. Can both be true at the same time?

Soon, I find myself face down on the bathroom floor.

He is sitting on top of me, pinning my arms to my side, while his knees dig into them on either side. His hands are around my neck.

Again.

I try to wrestle free.

His hold is stronger this time. He feels more in control. Me however – I freeze.

I am trying to signal to my arms and legs to do something, but they stop paying attention to me. Fear starts in a place seeded deep within me. But this time fear doesn't fuel me. I just lie there.

The bathroom was small. We are half in the doorway when he reaches into the hall and yanks the telephone wire I had stapled along the baseboard so I could have a phone in my office.

I had secured it neatly.

I had never imagined it would be used to kill me.

He wraps it around my neck.

He tightens it. Pulls back as his body leans back to get better leverage.

It should only take about two to three minutes before I am dead. That's all it takes. Two to three minutes before I take my last breath.

My cheek is simply resting on the floor, while a wire is about to kill me. My body goes limp.

At that very moment, I know I am going to die.

And, I start to cry, loud and powerful inside my head, although the room we are in, remains silent.

I cry for the life I wouldn't have.

I cry for my family in Norway that would never know what happened to their little sister.

I cry for all the things I never did, or said, or dreamt of for my life.

And, I whisper inside my head:

"I didn't even get to have kids..."

I want to be a mom. Not having my own mother – it made me realize I was supposed to be one myself.

Now, lying on that bathroom floor, the chances of ever becoming a mom, fades with each second. I resign myself to my own death. It was over.

He had set out that morning to come and kill me. He had planned it. Deliberate, viscous and by any means possible.

If that meant a telephone wire around my neck, pulling tighter and tighter, for as long as it takes, that is what he will do.

Only seconds remained, I was sure of it.

I closed my

eyes.

"It will be over soon" I thought.

And, when I open my eyes, I see her.

She's radiant and beautiful as she's standing in front of me, arms open, as if ready to finally hug me, for the first time.

Her eyes sparkle as her eyes meet mine. Her eyes are my eyes. The same shade of blue.

In truth, I do not know the color of my mother's eyes. I'm running towards her, my heart is beating so incredibly fast. I don't hesitate for one second. I don't question who this woman is. I don't have a memory of this woman.

But, at this moment, I know who she is.

All the things I grew up wondering about, are somehow a part of me as they are a part of her.

I don't hate her for not leaving me a note or a letter before she died. I don't question her love. I don't see the sick and worn out woman in the only photograph we have together with me as an infant.

Before me stands a woman who is strong, loved and vivacious.

Before me stands a woman who once was a little girl, then a wife and a mother. Before me stands MY mother, calling me home.

The past fades away. The story of her choosing me. The story in which she left behind three other children who loved her so much. A husband who worshipped the ground she walked on.

The guilt I have carried – I lived while our mother took her very last breath one month and three days later.

I stole their childhood and I could never live up to her image. I, the baby sister, could never replace their Mom. I took that from them.

None of it matters now. There was only love.

Nothing less.

Nothing more.

As I get closer, so close I can almost smell her, touch her, she stops, and screams.

"No! No, no, no!!!!"

I hear loud voices screaming, coming from somewhere in my head. Suddenly I heard them all — my mother, my father, my grandmother — their voices layered into one.

"Get up. Fight."

In an instant, I was no longer frozen.

I gasped.

Air.

With something beyond strength, I ripped my arms free, jammed my fingers under the wire, and tore it from my throat.

Now, I am the monster in the room.

Larger than human.

He shifted.

I rolled. I was on my feet. I don't remember how. I only know something primal had taken over. The lion in me woke up. I was no longer prey. I was enormous.

I believe God wasn't finished with me.

The same God I once raged at for taking so much from me.

That God gave me the strength to slip my fingers under that wire.

To pull.

To live.

He made one last weak attempt to keep me in the room with him, but it sounded pathetic. It sounded desperate.

At this point, he was desperate as he could see his control slipping away. Slowly, but it was beginning to unravel.

"Stay. Don't move," he uttered with a voice that lacked conviction.

I didn't wait for further instructions.

I moved.

I ran.

CHAPTER 28

Every Choice Has A Consequence

As my relationship with my first husband took root, I lost relationships with other people – quickly, or slowly, depending on who you ask. At the time, I figured it was just that typical *"new relationship bliss"* phase that we would eventually grow out of. I didn't recognize it as it was happening.

We never see it while we're standing in it.

From that very first night we met in his backyard, I knew my life was about to change.

I was there with my *"bad boy"* boyfriend, yet he and I both knew this between us was a temporary thing.

He left eventually after kissing me on the cheek, telling me goodbye. I don't think we ever spoke again. There was no future there to be had between that bad boy and me.

It had started after a break up with a wonderful young man, who scared the crap out of me by giving me a promise ring.

The *"promise ring"* guy scared me since I definitely wasn't ready for something that appeared so permanent.

I sometimes wonder what became of both of them.

The bad boy just wanted sex, which I honestly fought off as long as I could.

When he left that party did he in fact alter my future forever? Of course he did, but I didn't ask him to stay nor did I leave to go with him. It was simply what happened.

Choices don't always announce themselves as life-altering while they're being made.

Today's version of me understands that better than that eighteen year old girl could.

The man who got my attention was sixteen years older than me. It felt mysterious and exciting to have a grown man pay so much attention to me.

As we kept talking long into the night, soon we discovered we were the only two people left at the party.

Darkness set in his backyard yet neither of us seemed to mind as the conversation grew deeper and more personal.

It was the beginning of what was to come.

He would become my husband, my companion, my partner, my witness.

Then he was the one who would ultimately be charged with First Degree Attempted Murder and Unlawful Imprisonment.

That's the man I chose over the *"promise ring guy"* and *"bad boy guy"*.

I'm pretty sure I got it all wrong.

But, of course, I didn't know it then. How could I have known? There was no magic eight ball offering insight into what I should do.

"Ask again later" or *"Better not tell you now"* feel like foreshadowing.

There is no magic to be found in making life choices.

We alone decide who stays or who we allow in. We all seek some justification in every choice we make.

You can lie to yourself all you want, but we all want to know we are doing the right thing.

I ran away from a boy with a promise ring, and didn't follow a boy with a bad boy image.

Instead, I jumped all in with the mystery old guy.

Was it the right thing to do? As it turns out, it was not.

I did not want to hear any objections from anyone.

My whole heart had to fight so hard to survive later and still it just knew how it was always meant to love again.

Some people know how to play a part, like actors stepping into a role they sense you want to see. They mirror your hopes, your fears, your needs. At first, they tell you exactly what you long to hear, drawing you closer. Later, they become remarkably skilled at making you question your own reality.

The contradictions build so gradually you don't notice them forming—until you're already living inside them.

At first, my marriage didn't fail loudly.

It unraveled subtly and quietly, in ways that were easy for me to excuse and even easier to miss. When his mask finally began to slip toward the last two years of our relationship, it wasn't with rage or cruelty. It was control—carefully disguised as concern, guidance, even love.

It became clear what he wanted was not a partnership, but authority over my choices, my time, my confidence, my sense of self.

I was young, still learning who I was, and I didn't recognize the warning signs for what they were. Not then. Not for years.

Slowly over time I had become a smaller version of the girl I once believed myself to be.

The woman who had been curious, capable, and ambitious learned to second-guess her instincts – *my* instincts.

Isolation made it worse.

Cut off from outside perspectives, from voices that might have named what was happening, I lived inside a narrowed world where his version of reality carried the most weight.

In the beginning, it wasn't like I confided in many people either because frankly I didn't have the language for what was happening in our marriage. Over time, I learned to use my voice and started to share my frustrations with friends.

Always in private.

When he wasn't in the room.

His words were a careful mix of praise and poison. One moment, a compliment – just enough to keep me reaching for his approval. The next, a crude comment about my hair, offered casually, just to be mean and crass because he hated it once I cut it short.

A remark about the extra ten pounds, framed as concern when it was because he wanted me to be super thin. Which I was. About 135 lb at 5'10".

Subtle criticisms about my work which didn't stem from any truthful situation.

Each comment alone seemed small.

Together, they wore me down. My confidence eroded.

My joy dulled.

I learned to shrink in private.

I tried to soften my edges, to make myself more manageable. And all the while, I didn't see it as control.

I saw it as a compromise. As marriage. As love.

By the time I realized what had been taken from me, I couldn't pinpoint when it happened – only that the woman I once was felt very far away.

One day, when you have finally made efforts to leave the marriage, it all erupts. Heat, anger, and an emotional fire storm spills over into all the corners of your immediate surroundings.

You find yourself trapped physically by the mysterious man you chose all those years ago. You've been in that place with me and I don't mean to make you relive it.

I still do.

I will witness that moment of my life until the day I die.

Face down on the bathroom floor with a telephone wire around my neck.

It's only then that you realize the gravity of the mistake you made in that one choice.

To stay and not follow the guy who kissed you on the cheek before saying goodbye.

Today, I forgive that version of me.

It would be cruel not to forgive her.

Because, there was and never will be a magic eight ball to solve the mystery of choices.

That sure would be nice though, huh?

Then again, how do we learn from previous decisions as we move forward through life, if all was already decided for us?

The answer to that is, we don't wise up until one day, we just do. Because we lived a little. It includes pain. It includes heartache.

Only then, can we see what we didn't see before.

CHAPTER 29

A Skein Of Yarn

Take a skein of yarn and hold it in your hands for a moment.

Observe the carefully wound loops of yarn before searching for the end of the thread. It's thick and soft beneath your fingertips, and there's an excitement forming within you as you carefully plan what you are about to create from this simple material.

Then frustration surges in as you realize the end of the yarn is nowhere to be found. With a frown, you look a little closer.

It isn't where you expected it to be.

You turn the skein over in your hands, studying it from different angles, before finally pushing your fingers into its center and pulling gently, hoping to locate the hidden strand.

Eventually you manage to find it. Not the end you anticipated, but the end piece neatly protected inside the skein of yarn.

The blanket you are about to knit doesn't care where its beginning started. Stitch by stitch, its threads will fall into neat, patient lines as the blanket slowly grows and takes shape.

One day, it will lay draped over a sofa with someone napping underneath it. Perhaps one day be folded neatly at the foot of a bed, holding quiet memories of comfort and shelter.

Now think of a traumatic event in your life and ask yourself one question: does trauma bury itself so deeply over time that no matter which imaginary thread you try to pull, it still remains hidden inside?

I began pulling at that thread years ago.

Yet the more I tugged, the further inside it seemed to retreat. Some days brought progress, moments when light slipped through the darkness and I believed I had loosened the knot. Other days felt like I was sitting cross-legged on the floor, surrounded by loops and tangles, trying desperately to separate strands that refused to unravel.

Still, I kept working that skein, hoping to create something new. Hoping to create something better from what once felt unusable.

In life, there are countless threads connecting us.

Each friendship, each relationship, is built from moments that wind themselves together over time.

A spontaneous night out that stretches into early morning laughter. Sitting around a fire pit on a cool summer evening, listening to someone tell terrible jokes.

Then when that one friend inevitably stumbles, falls, and collapses into your Adirondack chair, breaking it, after one too many beers, everyone laughs until their sides ache.

A road trip to a seaside town with music turned up far too loud, windows rolled down and everyone excited about the adventures ahead.

These are the threads that weave us together.

Every time we revisit those memories, gently pulling on one colorful strand, we are reminded of the fabric that holds our lives in place.

When I pull at one of my life's darker threads, it becomes painful to discover what it holds. The strands tighten, almost as if his hands are around my throat once again.

The memories they hold are sharp and heavy, stitched with violence and betrayal, wound tightly together in a ball I spent years pretending did not exist.

It has taken time to find the courage to pull at those threads and they didn't unravel neatly in my hands.

Instead, they lay in a tangled mess at my feet.

I can't ignore the mess, I can't walk away from it or step around it. The threads demand I see them for what they truly are.

In a different world, the yarn would have remained perfectly wound and manageable. If only I had been more compliant, less confrontational and easier to control.

I believed the mess meant I had failed.

But healing, I have learned, does not happen in perfect lines or tidy stitches. It happens in patient, uneven rows, where some loops must be undone before they can be remade.

And slowly, with shaking hands and weary determination, I am still learning how to pick up those tangled strands and knit them into something that no longer defines my pain – but instead tells the story of my survival.

CHAPTER 30

Let Me Count The Ways In Which I Will Try To Kill You

When I reach the front door, this time he is delayed in reaching me. For the first time, he's not immediately behind me.

What I can only speculate is that he went into our bedroom to grab the wooden bat he is now holding. The silence feels wrong – too long and empty. I don't stop moving though, but something in me already knows.

Later, I will piece it together. He did stop in our bedroom to grab the bat. The same bat I had kept in the bedroom for protection since we had had a break-in a few months prior. How ironic.

Before I can understand what's happening, the impact comes. A brutal crack explodes against the left side of my head.

The sound is dull and deafening all at once.

For a split second, I think the world has broken open. It hasn't.

It's my skull.

I think my legs are about to give out on me as my vision blurs. I don't even feel pain at first – just shock, just confusion, just the sudden terrifying thought that this might be it.

Then the pain hits me.

It comes in waves, like the ocean's ebb and flow – almost calm but suddenly violent.

Pretty much like this entire morning has been like in fact. I taste metal. My mouth grows dry.

The room tilts and the floor feels like it's pulling me in while the ceiling is coming at me quickly.

I struggle to stay upright, my hands fumbling for something solid, anything.

I feel a sensation of warmth coming from the side of my head. I reach up to touch it, still trying to stay upright.

When I pull my hand back and place it in front of my face, my hand is covered with blood. My eyes grow wide as I take it all in. The reality of my life glaring at me, loudly, violently and brutally.

Quickly I shift my eyes from my blood covered hand, to him. About two, maybe three feet away from me.

So close, yet so far.

Not far enough, I think.

"Is this how I die?" I wonder.

"Is this bleeding hole to my skull, what will finally be how he kills me?"

He's standing there, holding the bat, ready to strike me again.

At first it feels as if he is frozen.

As if the whole world has in fact ground to a screeching halt. I hear nothing. Not even the hum a house makes that we all grow accustomed to. Not the freezer kicking on or a cat bouncing from the floor to the cat tree tucked in the corner.

Not a drip from a faulty faucet.

There is nothing.

Just for a moment, I feel as if I am in a trance.

As many other times this morning, I seem to leave my body. Hovering above it. Beside it. But not living in it.

It's the strangest feeling really. I hear my thoughts clearly yet it's as if I'm seeing them tumble out of my head in the form of words and sentences. If I were to reach out my hand, I could probably touch them.

Words hanging in the air with thought bubbles attached to them.

As quickly as this crazy notion hits me, I am dropped back into my body. Back into my skin covered in blood and bruises and painful agony.

I see him as if in slow motion, raising his hands up above his head once more, the bat about to make contact with my head for a second time.

His eyes are even darker now and his mouth is curled in a grotesque way I've never witnessed before. His breath sounds labored. But his body moves towards me, closing the gap between us quickly. Determination grows across his face and it scares the shit out of me.

And in that moment, I understand with the utmost certainty this isn't about stopping me from leaving.

"He's going to swing that bat again," I think to myself.

"I have to stop this…now!"

A voice rings out, loudly and fierce with intent.

It takes me a second to realize, the voice is my own.

"Stop it! Just Stop!"

CHAPTER 31

The Dog Park

The sun was setting somewhere on the horizon but this place wasn't filled with any of that wonder and amazement.

There was dirt and gravel that made up the makeshift path.

Darkness was falling. Rapidly. And, there was a man on that path, alone, walking a young German Shepherd named Vinnie.

The dog was unsure, following along, because dogs tend to be loyal. Vinnie couldn't see what was in the black garbage bags, in the wheelbarrow the man was pushing along. Yet, of course he knew what was in them.

Probably why he went along with the ruse to go "to the park."

As darkness fell, Vinnie would sit just a few feet away, as the shadows cast upon the man with the black garbage bags.

He watched as the man grabbed a shovel he had balanced on top of the bags as they had made their way, deep past the trails and into more wooded terrain.

Not far, Vinnie could see light from houses that circled the park. He could run for help, but Vinnie knew it was too late.

He knew what was in the bags. And, he didn't want to leave her.

He could smell her soap from the shower she took earlier that morning. The fruity scent of her hair.

But, he also could smell the scent of her dead remains. Stale blood.

When the man was finished digging, he turned for a second to make sure Vinnie was still there. As he threw each bag into the grave, Vinnie started to whimper, ever so slightly.

Vinnie was afraid.

He knew what he had seen.

Although he didn't understand any of it.

Why wasn't his mom moving? Or talking sweetly to him? Why wasn't she throwing his ball?

It was pitch black when the man and the dog made their way back to the parked car on the street. The man commanded the dog to get in.

The dog didn't move at first.

He had witnessed the man's eyes go black.

In a split second, Vinnie takes off running. Because a dog is only loyal when one is loyal to them. This man was not loyal to anyone or anything. He'd only stayed with the man to see where he was taking those bags. Because he was loyal to only one human, his mom who treated him with kindness and love.

Now, he had to find someone to tell.

Fortunately Vinnie didn't need to find someone to tell.

Fortunately what you just read was an imagined scenario.

Black trash bags, duct tape, a shovel and rope were found in my estranged husband's car. The reality of my possible demise does not escape me. I will never know what his ultimate plans were yet the seeds left behind leaves more to the imagination than not.

This was difficult to write.

I had to put myself there, in the dark and disembodied.

I cried for everything I had not accomplished. I cried for the fact that my family could have endured such a horrific reality not knowing what happened to me.

I got to meet Vinnie again, years later.

He was just a pup when we adopted him, yet the connection I had with him proved itself in time.

Vinnie was given a new home after. I couldn't keep him when I moved into a small apartment on the second floor.

Many years later, after having lost touch with his new owners (also my friends) and also for the fact, I no longer lived in the area, I stopped by Vinnie's new home.

I approached the house and there he was, barking away. I smiled. That felt familiar in an odd way.

He suddenly stopped. He remembered who I was.

My friends opened the gate and soon he was whimpering and rolling around on the ground near my feet.

I knelt down to pet him and started to cry. He jumped into my lap and licked my face, knocking me over. We sat together, legs and arms intertwined, reunited after over a decade.

I was laughing and crying because he hadn't forgotten me.

This chapter is dedicated to a sweet pup who ultimately didn't know what was happening around him that fateful morning, yet got to live a beautiful life. I am beyond thankful to my friends who took him in and loved him, when I couldn't.

I will never forget how we locked eyes through the bathroom window and he knew as well as I did, it was futile. If I wanted to survive, it was up to me.

We did it, Vinnie.

I made it. So did you sweet boy.

The last time I saw you all those years later, you kissed my face and looked at me as if to say: *"I'm glad I didn't have to smell your dead body. I'm so happy I got to smell your chamomile shampoo today..."*

CHAPTER 32

Is This How This Ends?

He does stop.

He doesn't strike me again, but he is still holding on to the bat.

His face is unreadable now. His mouth is a simple straight line and his eyes are void of emotion. My screaming for him to stop, has ultimately woken up something inside him.

He's not standing ready for another attack – he's almost nonchalant as he holds the bat at this side. His arms look weary.

I know this is only a temporary pause. I know he won't stop until I am dead.

So, I try a different approach.

I slow my breathing down and begin. Every fiber of my body knows I cannot get this wrong. My brain is connecting dots together so that I can execute this performance perfectly.

It has to be just right or he won't fall for it.

Deep breath in.

And, go.

"Hey honey, we have to stop this. We need to call and get some help here" I softly say to him as I reach for the bat in his hand.

As he grabs my arm with his free hand, I touch his upper arm and the bat falls into my other hand as he gives it up. I'm trying to hide the fact that my hand is trembling, but I don't think he notices. He too looks tired.

"Look at our wedding photo over there baby. Don't you see how happy we were at that moment? We can get there again babe – we just need to call someone and get some help, okay?"

I say this with as much love and compassion I can piece together. The hair on my arms is standing on edge as the words spill out of my mouth.

"We were happy once upon a time and I'm sure we can find our way back there baby" I continue, my voice dripping with pain.

"We just need to take a shower and get this blood off of us" he replies.

He has to be joking right now, I think to myself.

Absolutely ludicrous idea.

What kind of world does he live in where he thinks a shower to remove all the blood is going to fix this?

Even so, I gently stroke his upper shoulder and lean into him, kissing his neck. Convince him everything will be fine, I think to myself.

My stomach is churning, my heart is beating a mile a minute yet I force myself to slow it all down.

Everything is on the line right now and I have to get him to believe that I love him still. I continue to kiss his face, gently stroking his arm and move even closer to his rigid body. He seems to be softening ever so slightly.

"*Keep going…it's working."*

He starts to cry and before I know what is happening, he crumbles to the floor at my feet.

Soon he is on his knees, his body hunched over, his face near the floor.

Shockingly he is acting like a child and not a thirty-nine year old man who has just spent an hour and fifteen minutes trying to kill me. He covers his face with his hands, his shoulders shivering.

It's pathetic.

Why do I feel like he is not crying for me, but for himself?

This is an illusion.

He is still a monster.

He is no child; simply acting like one because he didn't get his way.

I take one last look at him as I calculate the distance between him and the door. It sinks in that I have enough room to open it. He isn't paying attention to me anymore as he seemingly is only thinking of how we are going to clean this all up.

I grab the door handle, turn it and pull. I hold my breath.

"Please God…keep him on the floor feeling sorry for himself," I pray silently. A gust of air hits my face, cooly and so I exhale.

Slow and steady.

The front door is open and I walk through it.

It's then my eyes go wide and I see what has been on the other side this entire time waiting for me.

The sun is high in the sky, causing light shadows in the yard from various trees and bushes. The sky is full of promise as I hesitantly take a few steps. Onto the landing, down the short steps and toward the street.

I suck some more air into my fragile lungs and realize I am finally out. He isn't following me this time. Not yet anyways.

Hope starts to grow, yet timid at first. I look down at my body.

My shirt is torn on the right side and my breast is exposed. I don't care and make no attempts to cover it up. I inspect further to find my bare feet are bloody and bruised.

My hands are caked with blood as well and my left hand is swollen so much it only faintly looks like a hand.

There are cuts in my left palm, with part of my insides, oozing out.

But I found the front door and I made it out alive.

"*Is this what freedom feels like?"* I think to myself in amazement.

I am running now, trying to get to the street to flag down some help. I need to find someone to help me.

But then, as I reach the last car in the driveway, I feel a hand grabbing my arm trying to pull me back.

"No, no, no…no more!" I scream.

I can't be sure if it was outloud or simply inside my own head but I can't fight any longer…

CHAPTER 33

Mommy Lives In A Picture Frame

Over the years, I have tried to imagine my mother when she existed outside the picture frame that sat on top of our wooden television in the living room. Before she was simply a name carved into a gravestone.

There isn't much to tell, because there wasn't much told to me. One day I would find out just a little bit more.

I was nine years old and had been admitted to the hospital about an hour from our hometown. I kept wetting the bed. The doctors searched for answers for quite some time before they finally found one. Eventually, there was a procedure done. And, that was it. I was fine.

On this particular day, my father had come to visit.

Soon we ventured outside to go for a walk. Get some fresh air. Escape the sterile smells that lingered in the rooms and hallways. In my child's mind, the building seemed incredibly large. As we exited through the automatic doors, I sensed my father was on a mission.

He kept walking much too fast and I was fighting to keep up.

I wondered where we were going and asked him as much.

"Come on, follow me, I want to show you something." he answered.

So, being the good little girl I was, I followed him. I would have followed him anywhere. He was my father.

Walking behind him, I started to feel a bit uneasy. Something just felt off. I sensed his sadness. I didn't realize it right away, but this felt important. Even at nine years old.

This was in fact the hospital that my mother had stayed during her cancer treatments and also where she died. Of course, treatments were disguised as simply making her comfortable as she moved toward the end of her life.

At nine, I didn't know this of course.

At fifty something, I still have questions in fact.

Coming out the main doors, my dad led me down the concrete sidewalk to the right. In front of us, I could see an older building of the hospital, separate from the main one.

It was wrapped in faded brick stone, slightly worn in places. Weathered from the sun and cold winters.

I see my father's back as he grows more distant from me, as his steps quicken ahead of me. My feet all of a sudden seem glued in place.

My father is nearing a door and is reaching for the handle to open it.

Instinctively, I knew I didn't want to follow him any longer.

He was showing me something on the other side, I didn't want to see.

Yet, I didn't have a choice. I figuratively unglued myself from the spot beneath my shoes and inched closer.

We made our way up one flight of stairs, then another and another, before he stopped at the landing and looked at me.

The pain I saw in his eyes at that very moment scared me more than anything ever had. I saw my father not as who he was at that moment, but about ten years earlier, at age thirty-three, facing a life without the love of his life, raising three teenagers and an infant, feeling the weight of the world on his shoulders.

He had been a man facing a life without the light my mother brought him. How would he ever figure out how to do even the simple things, like make dinner?

It's an unimaginable burden for anyone, much less a man over fifty years ago when the man was taught to never feel, never cry, to just do.

My father was very much just a person.

A person with fears, insecurities, and questions.

Sitting here today, I remember how much he loved and laughed during my lifetime.

But that day, at the tender age of nine, I saw the man whose entire world had been ripped out from under him when my mother died from cancer.

Just like that.

On a Thursday.

I wonder how he must have felt at that moment.

When there was no going back and nothing left to say. When he still had to face his older kids who were old enough to know their Mother.

Right before he opened the door, I knew exactly what was on the other side. Definitely not consciously, but his words left no question as to where we were. He pulled me closer to him, as we both huddled in the doorway.

Or did we go into the hallway? Possibly. But then he quietly pointed to one of the rooms over to our left.

"Your Mother died in that room, right there..."

You may be wondering what happened next?

I feel as though I ran all three flights of stairs, back outside, into the living world. But there were only two people there that day, one was nine and one is now dead.

All of a sudden, the woman in the picture frame had, in fact, lived a real life. Seeing where she died didn't suddenly make her closer to me.

And somehow, it did.

That was something tangible. She had been there. A real live person, not my mommy who lived in a picture frame.

She has always been and will always remain the woman who lives in heaven. For that reason, I would never know her moods, her characteristics, her likes and dislikes. Was she often angry or was she mostly happy?

What things made those things real for her?

I didn't know and will never know what her life looked like.

Today, in my fifties, having lived many years longer than she ever did, this not knowing lives in my heart.

It isn't a constant grief. It's more of a curiosity.

Did she hide in the closet to get away from things that made life heavy? I personally, as a mother, have done that.

I have failed in parenting countless times.

Did my mom?

Did she say the wrong things leaving scars far more reaching than it ever was intended? There is no way she was a perfect human being, although I feel she has been idolized in death.

I want to know all of her nuances.

The good and the bad.

Nobody smiles all the time.

I found myself back outside again. It's where the vision picks up for my nine year old self. The world out here looks the same as it did before my dad had opened that door and ushered me inside.

My mom wasn't in that empty hospital room of course. I couldn't run over and throw myself onto her weak body and ask her to stay.

"Don't go. Please don't go. Don't leave me…"

I would have surely cried out.

My father and I didn't talk about this after. The parent I am today, wonders why. I think I understand what motivated him.

His grief was lonely and he didn't want to sit in it alone. He wanted to share it with someone.

I happened to be that someone.

I didn't judge my father or fault him for missing her so much.

I, too, wished she had lived. Lived outside the picture frame sitting on the television in our living room.

His pain was a real pain.

My grief of never knowing her, makes me succumb to hiding in the closet sometimes. Or sit on the stairs looking at her photo that I have on my wall. She was incredibly beautiful. The natural kind of beauty that didn't require make-up.

She was my mommy that lived in a picture frame, yet she very much existed in the world.

Aside from that frame.

She laughed loudly, I imagine.

She baked cookies and fixed dinners. She mothered.

I also imagine, she did all those things really well.

Much more than a woman frozen in a picture frame.

CHAPTER 34

I'll Never Forget

I bury my tear-stained face into his furry neck and try to pull myself together. I know my oldest brother and my dad are coming to pick him up soon.

I don't want them to.

My father had flown back from a trip to California because he wasn't getting any better.

He was, after all, thirteen years old, which is a lot for a dog.

When I finally pull my face away, he looks at me with his deep brown eyes, steady and familiar, and in that look he seems to tell me it will be okay. Of course, he can't speak words.

He is our thirteen-year-old German Shepherd, Tell. And yet, it feels as though he is telling me everything I need to hear.

He is tired. He has done his job. He not only protected me and our family, but also worked as a security dog his whole life. I know as he is looking at me that he is ready for what comes next. My young heart is breaking.

Tell was there for so many chapters of my life. Through growing up and through all the seasons of my childhood. Through loss I didn't yet have language for. He was a constant.

Every day he would greet me after school. He would chase the swing in the side yard as I tried to go higher. I would gag in disgust as I put his meaty dog food on a plate at night for his dinner. I would laugh when he tried to sneak into the living room by sliding one paw across the threshold and pulling back instantly when my father gave him the side eye.

When the ground beneath shifted, he stayed – solid, loyal, predictable in the way only a dog can be. Loving me without question and protecting me without asking.

He once *"saved"* me from the lady at the butcher shop as she rushed out to see me in my buggy when I was a baby, I am told. My father standing at the top of the landing had to command him to let go and sit. She was not hurt by the way. I was his baby however, and there will be no touching today.

So, saying goodbye to him felt different, and yet painfully familiar. Although I had never known my mother and there were no farewells, I knew that death was permanent from a very young age.

No child should have that much awareness of the end.

Yet, I grew up simply knowing some day, it would all come to an end. He was also my childhood companion and I wasn't ready to watch him go.

I see now, how deeply this pattern would shape me.

Later, after my father's death the following year, loss would become something forefront in my life. Over all these years, loss has taught me to love fiercely but fearfully. To attach with my whole heart while quietly bracing for the moment it might be taken away.

In my mind, nothing lasts forever. And, much of the time, leaving and dying comes too soon. It has made me strong in some ways, but yes, it has left me exposed and vulnerable and ultimately tender in places I have yet to recognize.

This would be the version of me that would walk into marriage at the tender age of nineteen. I was a girl looking for permanence.

For safety.

That's a laugh looking back now.

Safety?

I was yearning for someone to catch me if I fell and not betray me by leaving me. I wanted someone to stay. I was a girl who was already carrying grief in her bones. That naive girl mistook commitment for protection and love for certainty. I was vulnerable in ways I didn't know how to name – trained by loss to hold on tightly.

Eventually it would turn into self-protection, whereas I would become the one who left – not wanting to be the one who would be left holding the bag. Anything to not be the one sobbing under the covers while watching a sappy romcom. If I left first, I could avoid some of the pain.

Tell licks my face and then rests his head onto my lap. There's a quiet acceptance we both understand.

His eyes met mine, calm and knowing. He had loved me his entire life.

And in his final act, he showed me something I was still learning – that love does not prevent loss.

It simply makes it worth it. It was another goodbye.

I would come to learn there would be many more. And I would grow to hate every single one of them.

CHAPTER 35

"I Am Just Going To End It For Me"

Suddenly I am being slammed up against one of the cars in our driveway and my body screams in pain. My body is exhausted and tired of this beating.

He tries to pull me back inside, but I fight him with every ounce of strength I still own. I beg him.

"Please just let me go, please..."

I scan his face. He looks at me with lifeless eyes.

"It's time for me to end this now" he says sternly.

"*Get back in that house,"* he added.

I had no plans of returning inside that house.
Again, I beg him to let me go. Then he does something unexpected.

He lets go and just looks at me blankly. No emotion in his facc. An emptiness in his eyes I've never seen before. I can't explain the darkness in them or what that might mean.

"I'm just going to go and end it for me" he says.

He disappears to the side of the yard and out of my sight. It is only then that I realize I need to go inside and grab my cell phone. I have no memory of going back to find it, but soon I am running towards the street, phone in hand, trying to call for help.

I am in the middle of the street, wearing a bloody white tank top, torn so that my right breast is exposed, gray sweatpants covered in blood, my dirty blonde hair drenched in blood from my head wound.

My hands are covered in blood, but at this point, so much time has passed, it has already started to dry.

I smell of fear, blood, dirt and sweat.

But at least I don't smell like death.

It isn't long before a car comes down the road from the right. I start to wave my arms around to make them stop. I am screaming, not even sure what words are coming out of my mouth.

"Help! Please! Help me!"

The car stops in the middle of the road about ten feet from me. I am standing just shy of the sidewalk so as to not get run over. I am shaking, barefoot and beyond terrified as I slowly move closer to the idling car.

I can't even see who is behind the wheel. It could be a woman or man for all I know. It didn't register then. And, now almost thirty years later, I still don't know the gender of the person in that car.

It doesn't matter. I just need a human being. We look at each other. And in that second I feel everything — hope, fear, shame, desperation — all crashing together.

At that moment I was not a twenty three year old grown woman but a little twelve year old girl who wanted nothing more than for her father to wrap his arms around her and keep her safe.

"Help me," I cry again to the faceless stranger.

The car continues to idle in the middle of the street. Nothing happens for a few seconds.

"My husband just tried to kill me!"

The words come out harsh and loud, yet silent and afraid simultaneously.

It is like if I don't say them fast enough, he will be there any second, to drag me back inside that house to "end it" as he had just said moments earlier.

I need this stranger to hear me. I need them to see me and do something.

I blink and when I open my eyes again, the car is gone, carrying the faceless stranger with them.

Only about thirty seconds passed from them stopping to them leaving me there, stranded in the road.

I don't blame the faceless stranger who chose to leave. Confusion lingered in their eyes. So did fear.

If our roles had been reversed, I don't know if I could have had the courage to help either. I was quite a sight. Like a character out of a slasher film.

Soon, panic rises within me.

I start to race all over the empty street, holding my cell phone and aimlessly pushing buttons that don't respond.

The pavement reached up to grab a hold of me. The clouds were going to come down and scoop me up and take me away.

There was ringing in my ears.

I hear people's voices all around me whispering yet I can't make out what they are saying. There is nobody there.

My legs feel weak and soon I know I have to sit down. I try to call 911 but the call never goes through.

I found out later, there had been a couple emergency calls from neighbors, although I have no idea what time those calls were made. From the carlier gun shot perhaps? From Vinnie barking in the back yard for so long?

Or did they call because of the second gunshot about to fill our neighborhood?

CHAPTER 36

Rain

The water falling from above me doesn't make much noise at all. It's when it lands, I hear it. Hitting the grass, the concrete, a child's plastic play toy, a garden canopy. I can hear the roar of a car engine on the busy road nearby long before I hear the sound of water splashing.

The rain itself is silent.

The air is crisp.

Cold and unforgiving.

Occasionally the wind picks up and pushes the rain sideways – two of nature's elements performing their own perfect dance.

It's easy to hide away indoors or under eaves and umbrellas when it rains. Children crave to jump in puddles laughing as water splashes up into their faces.

I wonder when that innocence turns into avoiding wet shoes and ruined hair?

When does life quietly sneak in and kidnap our childhood ways?

After I escaped the front door, eventually the rain season began. Did I step outside and dance beneath heavy gray clouds and simply dance? Did I embrace the child within my shattered heart?

I hope so.

I don't mind the rain.

It coaxes my body into less doing and more being.

It's a remarkable feeling.

Close your eyes.

Lean your face towards the sky.

Stretch your arms out wide, palms open, and feel the rain as it falls. Let it wash over you. Notice how everything fades away.

Breathe deeply. Cling to the fresh scent and soak in nature's quiet gift. Everything else becomes less urgent.

The dishes.

The laundry.

The school lunches.

Somewhere, someone turns up the faucet. The sky opens and releases its fury. My hair is quickly drenched, and my feet sink deeper into the grass beneath me.

Suddenly, I’m twirling, arms thrown wide.

I laugh in delight. I feel alive.

Because why not?

Why not laugh and dance with reckless abandon instead of grown-up obligations? Leave your mind open and willing to receive.

Let this simple moment be the beginning of something softer. Something healing. Let your heart be free. Let go of the pain. Let the rain cleanse what words cannot.

Tomorrow, the sun will rise again.

CHAPTER 37

Help Arrives At Last

The street stretches endlessly in front of me. Empty.

No cars. No people.

I am alone, half naked and afraid.

Suddenly a white van comes roaring towards me. It swerves onto the sidewalk. The driver barely puts it in park before jumping out.

It's a neighbor from down the street. I inhale sharply.

"What happened?" he says while his eyes scan my damaged body and blood stained clothes.

"He just tried to kill me," I say, nodding towards the house.

My neighbor gently grips me by the shoulders. He searches my face as if to confirm I am real. Alive. Stable enough for him to move.

Then he turns and runs towards the driveway.

"He has a gun!" I scream.

"Don't go in there!"

A second gunshot drowns out my voice.

The sound fills the silence and stops us both cold. It hung in the air longer this time. Not like the first shot, inside the house, that I had fired into the ceiling.

I immediately know this shot would have consequences. I was not wrong about that, I soon would discover.

My thoughts become more frantic with each minute. This was the beginning and the end. In one motion. Somehow, I felt it was finally over.

I was safe.

He couldn't hurt me anymore.

There would be no more pleading for him to stop.

No more pretending we could make our marriage work. I also would never know why. Not really.

I am not special.

Why throw your entire life away JUST so that you can end mine?

It is ridiculous to think because I was leaving, he would go to this extreme. It is ridiculous to think because he couldn't have me, he would try to kill me. My breath comes out in starts and stops.

I reach up and touch my neck, finally free from his grasp.

Blue and red lights soon blur my vision. People appear out of nowhere. I exit my body and hover somewhere above all these strangers in the street, just watching them.

My friend from up the street who was scheduled to come down at 11 that morning to help me move, suddenly was right there by my side.

She stares at me in shock, her face draining of color.

An aid car pulls up.

Then the police.

Then another ambulance.

More police.

All at once.

Within minutes, the street – a desolate and naked space just moments before – was filled with activity.

I could hear voices, yet I am unable to decipher their words. Neighbors come out of their houses and fill the street alongside so many strangers and emergency personnel. I become painfully aware of my own nakedness as I fumble to cover my partially nude body.

Overwhelmed by how quickly everything had shifted from silence to something else entirely. Like some scene from a movie and I was playing the part of a victim. Not that I in fact was one, because as I thought to myself, all this was not real.

Someone put a blanket over my shoulders. To cover up my nudity and provide comfort at the same time.

I sat on the steps of the aid car, on the side of the rig, staring into the ground in disbelief.

"I'm fine," I say.

"I don't need to go to the hospital."

The EMT's look at me with curiosity.

They know that of course I am far from fine. They gently coax me onto the stretcher.

All I needed was a hot shower and a week of sleep. All I needed was to get all this blood off my body.

I shivered then and I am shivering now at the thought. Denial at its finest.

I was not fine.

But the real reason I don't want to be carted off to a hospital in a blaring ambulance is simple. My inheritance is gone and my dear husband never bothered to add me to his health insurance through his job.

I don't have the money to pay for an ambulance ride.

And, really, there are just a few cuts and bruises, can't be anything major right? Never mind my left fist is swollen and I am about to realize my tongue will grow to the size of an orange in the next several days.

More than that, in the coming weeks, the whites of my eyes will be laden with blood vessels that have popped due to his strangulation attempts.

Sure, everything is fine.

Oh, sweet dear young me.

If I could reach back in time and wrap my arms around that version of me, I would take her face into my hands, look long into those blue eyes.

And I would whisper softly,

"Oh, darling girl...you survived. But you have no idea what it will take to heal."

CHAPTER 38

Reality Starts To Sink In

I don’t know if my neighbor rushed to his side.

Turns out, the second gunshot that had filled the air was him shooting himself in the chest.

While emergency personnel attended to me, they also attended to him.

A neighbor who happened to be a nurse got to him before emergency personnel arrived. She would later apologize after finding out what he had done. Of course, I understood that she was simply doing what she gave an oath to do. She was trained to do no harm. I couldn’t blame her for putting pressure on the gunshot wound he had inflicted on himself.

He was in bad shape.

Later I would be told he had placed the butt of the shotgun on a lawn chair, leaned over the barrel with it pressed to his chest, reached down and pulled the trigger.

The shot that rang out as my neighbor got to me in the street was a horrible act of cowardice.

I imagine it tore through his flesh, into his heart and lungs. His life was in danger. Later that evening, I in fact prayed he would simply die.

And, I am not ashamed to admit that.

I never saw him.

I know he was loaded into an ambulance and taken to the hospital. I too was taken away.

In which order, I don’t know.

As I lay there on the stretcher, the world zipping by in a blur, it was difficult to focus. I saw buildings, trees and even a blue sky out the small window. The world outside, blurred before my eyes.

I couldn’t focus.

Not on what I saw.

Not on how I felt.

The sirens were dull and loud, at the same time.

My body was being carried off to someplace safe. Yet my mind felt unfamiliar and scrambled.

This was the beginning of a life that would forever be known as after. What was before, would cease to exist.

This began with two people who no longer wanted the same things. One found herself sinking deeper into a marriage that failed her.

The other lacked the maturity to accept being dismissed.

Instead of understanding that some relationships end, he refused to let her go. It wasn't love.

It was an attempt to possess something that never belonged to him – because people do not belong to one another.

Sadly, two families became victims of his actions. It was no longer just about us. His family gathered around him, and soon mine would gather around me – two sides, standing on opposite sides of the same fence.

I wonder if he ever considered how the threads of that day would loop around so many lives. And even if he had, would it have made a difference? Would his actions have changed at all?

Did he EVER consider the lives his actions would touch?

And then I realize the harder truth – if he had, it likely wouldn't have changed a damn thing.

As the ambulance tires spun toward the hospital, the fog in my mind began to lift – not emotionally, but practically.

"I have four weddings this weekend," I kept saying.

"I can't miss them."

Even then, not fully aware of my injuries, I knew I couldn't fulfill those contracts.

My friend, who was supposed to help me move that morning, rode in front and began calling colleagues. By the time we arrived, she had secured coverage for all of my wedding shoots in the following days.

When she told me, my heart rate slowed.

One hurdle cleared.

There would be many more.

But this was the start. A step in moving forward.

At the hospital, things happened slowly.

I have no memory of coming in from the aid car and into a hospital room. I vaguely recall them removing my clothes and putting them into paper bags.

A nurse probably helped me into a hospital gown, gently moving my arms and limbs in order to tie the strings in the back.

I became aware of a detective sitting on a chair next to me at some point, ready to take my statement. I remember he was kind and never accusatory. He was gentle while speaking to me. His voice is soft.

"So, start at the beginning. He came to the house knowing you would be there?" the detective prompted.

I began telling him all the details as best I could remember. I gave him the back story to our failed marriage. I told him in detail all the ways my life was placed in jeopardy that morning.

It continued for a while.

For how long, I can't say.

The hospital staff came in and out of the room, as I shared my story. Taking my vitals, bringing me water.

I desperately asked if I could wash my hands. My face. The answer was a resounding and absolute no.

Photos would need to be taken before any of that could take place.

Unbeknown to me at the time, evidence of this crime would require documentation.

Exhaustion started to set in, yet I was told it was important to get as much detail down on paper while it was all still fresh in my mind.

"You are doing great. I am impressed at how much detail you are giving me. Keep going," the detective urged.

I kept going.

I recalled the baseball bat to my head.

The telephone wire wrapped around my neck.

His cold hands squeezing my throat.

Stabbing him in the neck in an attempt to escape out the front door.

While talking to the detective, I kept wondering why the staff still hadn't cleaned me up.

Again, they reminded me that they were waiting.

Injuries continue revealing themselves long after the violence ends. Mine kept appearing for days and lingered for weeks.

My voice grew tired.

Eventually, I had no more to share.

It was then someone came to take photographs.

I am looking at them now as I write this almost thirty years later.

It still hurts to see that younger version of myself frozen in those images. My blue eyes stare straight through the camera lens. There is a dullness there – and beneath it, a girl who is lost. A girl whose faith in humanity has been shaken to its core.

I see her fear and confusion.

But I also see a quiet strength behind those eyes. Without it, this would be a very different photograph.

Without that strength – without that fire – there would be no woman sitting upright, meeting the camera's gaze.

There would only be a cold, lifeless body on a metal drawer in some obscure morgue.

Let me just say, I know that strength, that fire constantly being stoked in my belly for lack of better imagery, is the difference between a photograph and a memorial.

I ask for a phone at some point. There is someone I need to call.

"Hello," says the woman on the other end.

"Mom, he tried to kill me!" I blurt out.

My mother-in-law is silent on the other end. I repeat what I had just said, my voice frantic yet trying to convey the seriousness of this day.

"Oh honey, if he wanted you dead, you wouldn't be talking to me right now," she says coolly.

I hung up the phone. I didn't speak to her again for about ten years.

That call went differently.

"Do I need to take out another restraining order?" I asked her.

"I don't think so. He's married and about to be a father. I don't think you have anything to worry about." she had said then.

"Do you remember our last phone call?" I continued.

"When you told me if he had truly wanted me dead, he would have killed me."

She exclaimed she didn't remember ever saying that and that if she did, she was sorry.

After a few more irrelevant pleasantries, we said goodbye. I never spoke to her or my father-in-law again. They had both been on the call.

They are gone now.

May they rest in peace.

They never tried to kill me.

Their son did.

After some time, a male nurse came in and finally stitched up my head. Seven stitches to the left side of my skull.

As I sit here thirty years later, I instinctively reach up and touch my scalp. For the fact that I have a head full of hair, it isn't visible. It feels bumpy and I don't need a visual to know what happened there.

My hands and feet were covered with various degrees of blood splatter. My face too.

Long dried tears had smeared the blood on my cheeks.

When did I cry? In the ambulance perhaps?

When the world was passing me by and the gravity of all of this set in – is that when I allowed myself to cry?

The streaks are obvious in the photographs taken of me that day. My hospital gown was adjusted to photograph my nude back.

My profile with my tongue sticking out. Growing in size already.

My legs and hands are photographed separately from the rest of my body as I'm now asked to sit up in the hospital bed. They move in close to accurately document the injuries from various areas of my body.

The blood has dried into a dark shade of red – almost black.

My hands are covered in it.

I am desperate to wash it away as I go through the motions. Reality is beginning to set in now.

My hands get stitches as well. Two areas that are still visible today. Some days, I notice them. Most of the time, they go unnoticed.

It felt like hours passed in slow motion.

A constant cycle of hurry up and wait. There was treatment and questions. More questions, then the stitches.

When I was finally told I could go home, I knew there was no home left to return to.

CHAPTER 39

How Do We Find Humor After Trauma?

After the dust settles and life somehow finds a new rhythm, how do we find humor after trauma? When life keeps moving forward because that is simply what it does, how do we allow ourselves to laugh again?

Does it take hours? Days? Months? Years? Twenty years?

And more than that, how do we let ourselves off the hook so we don't keep falling victim to the same moment over and over again?

I have no idea.

You could have asked me thirty years ago, and you could ask me today – I still don't have a clear answer.

But at some point, we do laugh again.

Sometimes at the most inopportune times.

Sometimes not because we want to laugh, but because we don't know how else to respond. Sometimes it is simply reflex.

A strangely comforting one.

Science tells us laughter releases endorphins. And perhaps when the world as we know it is unraveling at every seam, laughter is when we need those endorphins most.

When the life you had carefully mapped suddenly tears into pieces. When your trust has been flattened like it was hit by a semi-truck. When your belief in what is good and kind and true shifts so violently you no longer recognize the landscape.

That is when laughter may arrive uninvited – at the worst possible moment.

I was lying in that hospital bed, fog settled into my mind.

Shock — not physical, but mental.

Thoughts racing without order.

My heart felt like it was pounding loudly enough for everyone in the room to hear.

Somewhere deep in my stomach, I already knew my life had permanently changed. This would stay with me. I wasn't wrong.

Then came rage. A feeling I had never experienced before. Who the hell did he think he was? Why did he think that if he couldn't have me, nobody else could? He was sixteen years older than me — and I was only twenty-three.

He should have known better.

A separation. A divorce. Those are endings.

This was something else entirely.

I wanted to stay silent. Then I wanted to talk endlessly. Then I felt as if once I started crying, I would never stop. I imagined myself later, standing in a grocery store aisle, suddenly sobbing. For no reason. For every reason.

I held it in. I wasn't ready for the grocery store breakdown yet.

I didn't know then that it would come one day. I would abandon all my dinner ideas and drive home with only a bundle of bananas.

After hearing everything, the detective had said

"Most women are killed within fifteen minutes. You fought him for an hour and fifteen. You should be damn proud of yourself."

And I am.

That intention to live has never left me.

Neither has the ability to laugh.

That first laugh came only hours later, in that hospital room.

At the worst possible time.

I have often wondered why I laughed – truly giggled.

Was I afraid that if I didn't laugh at that moment, I might never laugh again?

I'm no psychologist, but the mind protects itself in curious ways.

And in that moment, while the photographer tried to capture my face, I laughed.

I simply laughed.

Inside my head, I scolded myself. What is wrong with you? This is not funny. It wasn't. But both the photographer and detective remained patient, which makes me think this was not the first time they had seen a victim laugh when they weren't supposed to.

The photograph they captured shows no trace of laughter.

Only the truth of what happened that morning.

People who see it still cringe.

Years later, I think I understand why I laughed. Sometimes laughter is the body choosing relief over collapse.

There is something almost absurd about having a portrait taken while looking like you narrowly escaped death.

So when do we find humor after trauma?

We find it when it finds us. That wasn't a joyful laugh.

But the fact that laughter existed only hours after almost dying tells me something I couldn't understand then.

Some part of me already knew I was going to be just fine.

Not for a long time.

But, one day I would be just fine.

CHAPTER 40

I'm Back In The Shower

What I had called home for six years, had not been released by the police department yet.

It was a crime scene.

My friends brought me to their house instead.

There, for the first time since that early morning, I would be able to shower and wash the blood from my body.

The hospital had not kept me overnight, probably due to my lack of health insurance.

Nor did they offer to clean me up.

Just as well I suppose.

I caught my reflection in the steamed mirror and didn't quite recognize the woman staring back at me. My eyes were dulled by shock, but still open. Still holding on.

It had been less than eight hours after my first shower that day. And here I was, about to take another.

So much feels different now. Everything felt unfamiliar.

A different house. Four walls. Doors and windows. Someone else's home. Here I didn't feel trapped. I didn't feel the urge to climb out of the bathroom window or fight my way to the front door.

This was safe.

I can't remember what I wore leaving the hospital although I clearly remember what I wore before I ended up there: white tank top, gray sweatpants, panties and no bra.

I removed the clothes my friend had brought me in the hospital. They landed in a heap at my feet as I tried to steady myself.

Steady myself for what is to come next. Seeing in the mirror what he had done to me.

I stood for a long time before making my way into that shower.

Before me stood a naked woman. Shivering slightly in the cool air before turning on the water.

Bruises appeared more deeply now. The whites of my eyes showed early signs of broken blood vessels. My hair was matted with dried blood. Blood smeared my face.

I let my eyes travel lower – dried blood on my hands, my legs, my feet. It was terrifying. I was hunched over, yet trying to stand up tall. Shoulders back. Chest forward.

But, everything ached.

The woman in the mirror was a stranger staring back at me.

I searched for the young woman who had woken up that morning believing she knew her life. She was gone.

Never to be found again. An irrevocable change.

The childish games and the desire to always trust, now would be a bit skewed.

A bit jaded.

I didn't know it then. The jaded part would come much later.

Standing there that evening, tears started to fall down my face. Without a sound. I didn't scream. I possibly even held my breath for just a moment.

Was what I was looking at real? Was that really me?

More blood seemed to smear my cheeks with each silent tear. I couldn't find my voice. There were no heart wrenching sobs along with the tears. Just this tremendous pain from within, streaming down my face.

Quietly.

My throat started to swell up like there was a huge plum stuck inside.

This was a quiet pain I would have to bear for the rest of my life and in that moment, I knew I could NOT let it define me.

No time for loud and dramatic sobs. Not right now. I wasn't ready.

All of a sudden I was terrified, standing there. I had this beating heart inside me, yet I felt as if I was not really there at that moment.

Maybe I was at the morgue, under a white sheet with a tag attached to my toe with my name on it. Maybe me standing there at that very moment was the dream and the reality was that he had actually killed me.

At some point, something told my brain to get in the damn shower. The mirror had fogged up and there was nothing left to see in the reflection.

My hand moves the shower dials to adjust the water temperature before slowly lifting each leg over the tub and inside. When I eventually would do so, my legs felt heavy, like a couple of hundred year old tree stumps soaked in concrete.

I can't say it was a great shower. I can't say it was terrible either. What I can say is that I will never forget the smell of my own blood. Metallic and clinical.

As the water cascaded over me, it felt as if every inch of my body was still covered in it. In my mind, the tub filled to the rim with bright red blood. My feet waded in it.

All imagination.

Cruel nonetheless.

Slowly the drain sucked all the blood down, yet the smell would remain for every shower for many weeks to follow.

I started buying fragrant body washes. Washed my hair twice each morning. To feel clean.

Once the steam in the room felt unbearable, I shut the water off. I stood there for a moment before stepping out. The soft bath mat underfoot seemed to ground me as I dried off. I towel dry my hair and hesitantly wipe a section of steam off the mirror.

This time seeing my reflection, I see something less dramatic. I see determination.

I am bruised and battered, yes, but I no longer have a face streaked with blood. My hair is void of the bloody tangles. It hangs loosely and gently now, framing my face.

I smell clean.

I attempt to smile at the girl in the mirror. She smiles back at me as she takes a deep breath.

"Everything is going to be ok," I whisper.

I dress in clothes my friend had given me and leave the bathroom, closing the door behind me.

CHAPTER 41

Silk Pajamas

When you find yourself standing on the highest mountain, surrounded only by dark clouds, thunder looming in the distance – alone, naked, exposed and confused – all you want to do is find your way back down from the mountain.

Through narrow pathways.

Over sticks and stones.

Blackberry vines catching your ankles as you stumble forward.

It stings.

It bleeds a little.

But you keep moving.

You think you know the way back.

At least you hope you do.

As I sink into the soft sheet spread across my friend's sofa, I try to wind back time. Or force it forward – quickly – just to get through it.

I place my head on the pillow and pull the blanket up around me.

I pray for sleep. To quiet my mind.

If only for a few hours, I need to remove the diabolic images from just a few hours ago. I need the movie reel playing on a relentless loop to pause.

When everything has inexcusably been taken from you, you find solace in the kindness of others.

You find comfort in the silk pajamas and robe a friend brought over for you.

Because as she said, this is a time to still feel beautiful and lovely – like only a silken piece of fabric can allow.

As my hand gently touches the fabric, it feels smooth and forgiving.

It's as if I was given a new skin temporarily.

For a brief moment, I smile at the gesture.

It feels nice to feel beautiful again.

Not the bruised woman I discovered in the bathroom mirror earlier that evening.

Before long, I can no longer keep my eyes open.

With a tear stained face, I drift into restless sleep.

The movie reel pauses.

Only for a moment.

A scream fills the room.

My eyes fly open and I realize the scream was mine.

My friend is there instantly, wrapping me in a warm hug.

Fear had engulfed my dreams I sadly realized. I shouldn't be surprised. I had fallen asleep, praying he would just die.

Perhaps my dreams were payback.

There was no escape.

No reprieve.

But there were silk pajamas.

Lending me a new skin until I could regrow my own.

CHAPTER 42

What's Next?

There's a calmness to the house now as I unlock the front door.

I wasn't expecting that. The last time I was here, I was in a state of terror. Fear that I would never make it out.

Now, as I am standing facing inwards, my body isn't reacting by trying to flee. It smells musty and heavy as I slowly make my way through the living room and towards the kitchen. I can hear the hum of the refrigerator and shudder to open it to see remnants of what used to be food inside.

There likely isn't anything worth finding anyway. I had lived here alone for two weeks and couldn't remember the last time I had gone grocery shopping.

I look around and take it all in. I take a deep breath as I walk further through the house.

Boxes, furniture, and belongings are strewn everywhere.

Yet nothing here can hurt me anymore.

Most importantly, he can't hurt me.

He is locked up awaiting prosecution for what happened here in this house.

Attempted Murder in the First Degree.

Unlawful Imprisonment.

Those are his charges.

He can't yell at me anymore, telling me he doesn't like what I cooked for dinner last month. He also can't yell at me to get the laundry done or clean the bathroom. I won't be doing any of that in this house ever again, I think to myself.

Near the front door, a bloody handprint stains the wall.

My hand.

I stare at it in disbelief. For all that it represents. For all the proof anyone would need to understand what happened.

I reach out and barely touch the outer edges of it. A shiver goes up my spine and I decide to walk away from it.

Black fingerprint ink is smeared throughout the house as well. It looks like a crime scene – worse, perhaps – because this space was filled to the brim with his ridiculous antiques and now the moving boxes I had packed in preparation for leaving as well.

How I wish I could have just moved into my new apartment the day before he showed up intent on killing me. Knowing what I know now, all these years later, it wouldn't have made a difference.

He would have found a way regardless. I have no doubt about that. I make my way down the hall towards the bedroom.

Oh, the bedroom.

I have a physical reaction when I stand in the doorway. There are mental images just under the surface of my eyelids and I force my eyes to remain open so I don't have to see them.

This room gives me pause.

Even thinking back on it today, almost thirty years later, it holds the key.

A bedroom is a person's sanctuary and where we feel the most relaxed. Where we rest and prepare for another day. Where we make love. Where we shed our clothes without a care in the world. Where we exist in private moments, never expecting unwanted eyes.

This is the room he chose.

I hear an echo of his voice if only for a brief second.

"If I can't have you, nobody can..."

I back away slowly and open the etched glass door to my office.

I sit at my desk in my office for what feels like a really long time. In reality it was probably no more than a couple of minutes.

I find it difficult to remain still in this house.

This room, unlike all the other spaces in this tiny house, is barely a mess. Boxes line the floor as I had already begun packing in here.

This house is now just a hollow frame with windows and doors.

Not a home.

Was it ever?

I always wanted it to be.

Isn't that what we all dream of anyhow? A place we land at the end of each day that keeps us safe from the outside world.

The world can be cruel and relentless, but we imagine our homes as shelter: soft light, a whimsical piece of art above a crackling fireplace, a blanket draped lazily over a sofa, an oversized, slightly chipped mug of coffee resting beside a stack of books waiting to be devoured.

A place where the outside world cannot come in and destroy our peace.

Walking through the house in the aftermath, I understand now that safety isn't always about what we keep out.

Sometimes it's about recognizing who we never should have let in.

I find myself standing in the small kitchen and impatiently search my mind trying to recall time spent here with my husband and our pets. We didn't cook often. Not that I can remember.

We would usually go out to dinner.

Countless regular restaurants would prepare our family dinners.

A family of two.

He would make the occasional Lasagna which I grew to hate. I would make my Norwegian spaghetti which turns out he didn't like either. Peach cobbler? He made that sometimes and it was good.

I try to imagine lazy days spent on the sofa watching tv, but it only brings with it further confusion. Have I truly blacked it all out? Would anyone blame me?

As I sit here now, thirty years later, I am still trying to picture our life together in an effort to paint a complete picture of that life all those years ago.

I ran across some photos recently and it gave me chills. I see him on the sofa with our cats. He took one of me sitting at the kitchen table using my typewriter, probably for a college paper. There were more photos of him than me.

I was documenting a life I thought.

Yet he rarely did because what? He didn't care enough to take photographs of his wife?

Which is such a contradiction as he claimed he loved me too much to ever let me leave him.

All those photos have been carted off to a landfill somewhere. I have no desire to keep documentation of a life that it turns out was all a charade.

A lie.

A life filled with broken promises and seven stitches to my skull.

Friends are joining me soon so I head back into the bedroom. I have to continue packing.

I know this house can't control me anymore than he can.

As soon as my things are moved, I can release it back to the landlord.

And, that is what I plan to do.

Even now, as my body still aches from the brutal beating I received, I have work to do.

I spotted one of my favorite hoodies and put it on. It feels kind, forgiving and safe. And then I get to work.

Things don't pack themselves.

A life can't move forward if we remain still.

CHAPTER 43

Picking Up The Pieces

The craziest part, after everything that had happened, was that I was still the one left to pick up the pieces.

The world did not pause for my pain.

The mundane tasks of moving forward with my life waited for no one. There was no time to crawl into the fetal position pretending this had not happened to me.

There was no time to fall apart and mourn. Grief had to stand in line behind necessity.

I wanted to mourn everything at once – the marriage, the lies, the person I thought he was, the person I thought I was. I wanted to mourn the version of love that didn't come with violence. I even wanted to mourn my faith in people.

Instead, I caught myself praying he wouldn't survive.

A brutal thought, but an honest one.

Pain does not make saints of us.

He lived.

Half a lung gone, but alive.

He was sent from a hospital bed straight to jail. And just like that, his story paused while mine had to keep going.

I was twenty-three. Alone in a country that started to feel like less of a home.

No family to fall into.

No time to wonder if I was capable.

I moved forward because there was no other direction to go.

What I couldn't understand was how it was possible for so much hate to grow where love once lived.

I ended up hiring an auction company who brought in a crew to get the house, yard and small shop cleared out.

Everything was moved into their storage facility to be placed up for sale in order to pay off some of the marital debt.

Because of his attorneys and family, this auction continually kept getting delayed. It was a legal battle that lasted for months. Although I had brought my inheritance into the marriage, which was substantial, they didn't see it fit that I should be in control over selling items that previously belonged to him.

Which honestly, was just junk. Yes, perhaps there were some antique furniture pieces, but there were so many broken down engines, boat parts, car parts, tools, some furniture and yet the bottom line was it was not worth much.

He had spent my inheritance on things and furniture we did not need. It was his obsession. He would randomly show up with a 1950 (or was it 1963) Buick, or two broken down Jettas he planned to make into one vehicle. Outboard motors he would tinker with for hours out back in his cluttered mess of a shop. He would then sell it to somebody, yet never give me back the money I had used to buy it in the first place. He would just go out and buy more junk.

I would never understand how our house had become this insane place filled with things.

I swear there were three large wood buffets in our tiny living room lining the walls. So much furniture it was difficult to move through the place.

It was one of the reasons I wanted out.

Deep down I knew I was simply one of his prized possessions, like the furniture overspilling in every nook and cranny in our home.

Not his wife.

In the space between our separation and that fateful day, he had in fact taken several pieces of furniture away.

I didn't even bother asking him what he did with them. I couldn't care less. He could have everything he had bought with my money, as long as he was no longer in my life.

After it was all said and done, and after having to pay thousands of dollars in storage fees to the auction company, I was left with a small chunk of change. I paid off some business debts from my photography business which had fallen behind due to his insane spending habits and consolidated the rest. It took me about four years to pay it off, close to forty thousand dollars.

I moved into the new place I had already put a deposit on, and I think for the first time in my life, I was in love with my home.

It didn't smell funny or was packed to the ceilings with nonsense. It felt like freedom.

I made one bedroom my office, with my desk and computer as well as a new futon which would work well for guests. A large bathroom was located right next to it.

Everything was shiny and new. Everything had a place and there were large closets to store work equipment for my business.

The master bedroom was filled with just what is deemed normal.

A bed, a couple of nightstands, a couple of table lamps and a television. No stacked boxes of random things sitting on top of bulky buffets or dressers.

The walk-in closet was huge. Lining two walls in a hallway that led to the master bathroom. It felt like pure luxury.

I took a bubble bath every night for a week after moving in.

On the deck, I created a beautiful space filled with flower baskets. Two chairs and a small round table. It became my outdoor sanctuary every morning enjoying a cup of coffee.

Each piece of furniture or artwork or thing had intention.

It felt promising to be in control of what my new safe place looked like. I didn't have to ask for permission from anyone.

I still had nightmares though.

Those would interrupt my sleep for a long time.

As I was trying to create a new life for myself, there were still things to take care of.

Divorce proceedings, lawyers, selling of property, the auction company. Getting the house we had shared empty.

I was left to pick up the pieces.

Not just financially, but physically – walking through the house we had lived in, deciding what to keep, what to discard, what to set aside for his family. Each object felt loaded. Each decision felt too big for someone my age.

It was a daunting task. Looking back now, I don't know how it all got done.

I have no memory of strength or strategy. I simply moved through it because I had to.

One motion after another. Survival on autopilot.

At least I didn't have to scrub the blood from the walls.

I heard his family ended up cleaning the house. No confirmation on that but at least it wasn't me.

The bloody handprint, the stains near the front door that were mine, told the story without words. Anyone could have walked in and known something terrible had happened there.

I paid the landlord for an extra month, emptied what I could with the help from the auction company as well as a few friends, handed the keys back, and tried to wipe my hands of the whole life I had lived there.

I was done. Or at least, that's the word I used then.

But "done" is far too small a word for what lived inside me that summer. I wasn't done – I was depleted, gutted and operating on fumes.

The system is not built to carry victims; it quietly hands them a bill instead.

Debt settles in everywhere – emotional debt, financial debt, psychological debt.

Trauma sends invoices for years.

And all those debts collected interest for far too many years afterwards.

CHAPTER 44

He Burned The House Down

As I sat in the conference room with a slew of important people on either side of me, it was as if I was watching my entire life burn to the ground.

The only thing was, although it felt accusatory towards me, I was not the one who had set the fire. I had not lit the match and figuratively tossed it over my shoulder, watching the house ignite. As everything slowly turned to ash, I was hovering above it all, absent from both body and mind.

The flames quickly took hold of curtains, of the sofa, the art and photographs on the wall.

It didn't discriminate as it crept along the floor, causing destruction in every corner.

They all looked at me.

The young girl from Norway who had escaped that house. Them?

They were defense attorneys, prosecutors, interns, detectives and note takers all there to take my official statement.

The story was already clear in my mind, yet here I was, alone in a world so foreign it felt absolutely terrifying.

"So, let me get this right. When he hit you over the head with the baseball bat, did he use all his strength to do so?" the arrogant man seated to my left asked.

He was dressed in an expensive business suit, overpriced shoes and holding a pen hovering over a yellow legal pad. I inhaled sharply, locked my eyes with his and simply said, "Yes. Yes he did."

"You are taller than the defendant. Do you really think your life was in danger?" this man, a complete stranger continued.

Again, the answer was a resounding yes.

Seething anger began to take hold of me from somewhere deep inside.

It began slowly in the nook of my belly, traveled up my body, wrapping itself around my throat and squeezing.

Again, I was being choked.

Again, his power took hold as he once more attempted to kill me.

He was not there in that room amongst these people, yet they were doing the dirty work for him. How is it appropriate for a survivor to travel back countless times to relive an experience she never initiated? To have to set words to the agony of her reality? It felt as if she was the foreman on a jury that would later convict her for her stupidity.

I told myself it had been stupid to marry a man whose greatest fear was losing control of someone he believed he owned.

Before I sat in that conference room, traffic was light. It was a different time, almost three decades ago, and as with many cities, it has grown a lot since then. Traffic today is not what it was back then.

Yet, my hands were still gripping the steering wheel as I maneuvered the freeway, locating my exit and finding the correct city streets.

I tried to calm my anxiety.

Not just because I was driving on unfamiliar streets, but for what was ahead of me that morning. I told myself this was nothing more than a simple meeting.

Regrettably, it would always be more than that. It was too much for any person to navigate all by herself in a land that didn't raise her, but stole her innocence.

There was no GPS on my smart phone or navigation system built into my little '84 Toyota Corolla telling me which exit to take off the freeway or which street to turn onto.

Nonetheless, I turned the volume down on the country music radio station as I neared the county prosecuting office building.

After parking, I unbuckled my seat belt, exited my car and made my way to the conference room. The elevator seemed to lag on for miles and the palpitations in my chest almost broke me.

My mind told my legs to move towards this meeting and to face it head on. The little girl in me wanted to run in the opposite direction and be anywhere but there.

Minutes turned into hours answering their questions. Most of which were frankly ridiculous. Yet, I suppose they were also searching for the truth.

What actually happened inside that house on 73rd street?

Tell us.

We are listening.

"But are you really?" I wondered.

I was trying to explain the fear my estranged husband had inflicted on his much younger wife. Fighting for justice in a system that felt designed to fail me. Pulling their imaginary hands from my neck as they tried to choke me one more time. I was fighting to keep the bat from hitting my skull.

Yet it felt like there was one blow after the other until there was nothing left of my skull to shatter.

I was fighting to be seen. And heard. Something my husband had grown incapable of doing. I had become an object and a possession, although looking back, perhaps I never was anything different. I had been too naive to see it.

His defense attorney wanted to beat this story to death.

The bruising around my neck, the popped eye vessels, the skull laceration from the baseball bat, the hand slammed in the door, the broken teeth, the telephone wire around the neck, the shotgun he tried to shoot me with, the cuts on my hands and feet.

He wanted to go over all of it.

This man had the audacity to ask;

“In your opinion, did he use all his strength when he hit you in the head with a baseball bat?”

What kind of strategy was this?

"In your opinion, when he hit you in the head with a baseball bat, did he intend to kill you?"

"When he wrapped the telephone wire around your neck, did he pull it really tight or just slightly tight?"

"I understand he told you that you were going to die. Did you feel he meant that or was he simply trying to frighten you?"

What his defense attorney did not ask me about was my broken heart.

My shattered vision of the world and the people in it. He didn't foreshadow that one day, I would be so jaded that I couldn't really trust again. How do you truly allow someone in after this?

Would I always be looking over my shoulder wondering how someone who is supposed to love you, will ultimately hurt you if they don't get their way?

This man, disguised in his fancy suit and ridiculous shoes, might not have been the man who tried to end my life, yet he seemed to have an appetite for drama.

He made me fight for my truth when clearly, this was not rocket science, and his questions were only created to make me feel less than.

Feel like nothing.

His intent was to make me feel as if this was all a big misunderstanding. And, that it was all my fault.

Make that make sense.

You can't.

It became obvious, his defense attorney was made from the same cloth as the man I once had been married to.

It takes a special type of person to treat me as that man did that day. By doubting my memory of the event that brought us all there that morning, he ensured my pain would linger for decades to come.

It was not his responsibility to take it all away – nobody could – but he kept throwing gas on it, followed by a lit match, then another.

That is not what human beings were created to do.

I don't care what circumstance or scenario. There comes a time when perhaps fighting for your own cause, in this case, your client, it just needs to stop. When you've taken it too far. Far beyond the scope of defending actions that were never defensible. They can't be justified no matter how you attempt to twist the truth.

I leaned forward in my chair.

My eyes met the overpriced lawyer's gaze, my expression flat, not smiling and attempting to not show fear.

This man could never hurt me.

I spoke his name, first name in fact, because I felt that would make him listen.

"I hope you are listening because I am only going to say this once."

He sat up, leaned forward, his eyes quizzical.

Out of the corner of my eye to my right, the prosecutor and detective sat up just a little. *"Who was I all of a sudden? Was that my voice speaking loudly and with bravado?"*

My heart was beating out of my chest. I continued, having had no preconceived notions of this.

"I am twenty-three years old and we can sit here for another two hours if you would like. You can ask me if I think he used enough force to possibly kill me when he hit me in the head with the baseball bat, over and over again. The answer will always be the same. When he hit me in the head with the bat, his intentions were to kill me. This man tried to kill me. No matter how you want to twist and turn it around, grab a broom and sweep it under the rug, it will not change the fact that he tried to kill me. I am twenty-three years old and I pray this never happens to another woman although I know there will always be men out there just like my husband, thinking their wives are property. Right now, I am done. I am getting out of this chair and leaving

this room. I am done sitting here being made to feel small and insignificant. Nothing I did brought us all here today. His attempt to kill me brought us here and I am done answering ridiculous questions trying to undermine my experience and the truth."

My heart would not stop racing.

I was convinced every person in the room heard it, yet I pushed my chair back and walked to the back of the room and exited through the door on the right.

Once in the hallway, I leaned up against the wall and closed my eyes as my head rested against the marble-like surface. I tried opening my eyes, only to see a sea of shadow and light. I closed my eyes again and inhaled slowly.

Everything will be okay, I tried to reassure myself. It had to be.

It felt like several minutes, but probably only a minute passed before the detective on my case was standing next to me. He looked at me with a combination of pride and sadness as he told me I did a great job holding my own, yet unfortunately I would be required to come back in.

I was shaking like a leaf.

The kind you do after a confrontation with another human being. I realized they were just doing their job, but I was so angry at that man who had spoken to me as if this was my doing.

The firetrucks are miles away putting out other fires and will arrive when they can. They won't get there in time to save anything. The house is ash and dust and nothing will rise from it again. Any hopes and dreams of babies and happiness that lived in that house have evaporated.

Over time, flames dull and only embers remain. Like a memory fades through the years as we create new memories that replace the previous ones.

I wish I could tell you the rest of what happened that morning, but I can't.

I don't know if they made me go back into that room yet if I truly wanted to know, I could request documentation.

I don't need documentation.

Truth doesn't require one.

Any further questioning was noise – beneath the truth, unworthy of it.

Because the truth was already out there, and no matter what ridiculous question the man in the suit would or could ask next, it paled in comparison to my gut speech.

My gut speech was authentic. Every question answered prior to it, was also authentic. If anyone in the room wanted to play pretend, those notions had been put to rest.

I wasn't a wallflower.

I was verbally manipulated by my husband, isolated from friends and family he didn't approve of, but I was no wallflower and I was more than ready to stand up for the truth as to what happened to me.

No man in a tailored suit could rewrite that story. No hourly fee could outbid the truth.

Not even for a defense attorney whose job depends on bending it.

CHAPTER 45

It's 3 AM And I can't sleep

The girl looking back at me from the mirror isn't me. It may seem like it's the same person from a little over a week ago, but that's a lie.

I've changed.

The girl I see, lit only by the weak glow of a small lamp on the counter, is bruised from the inside out.

I study her as if she is a stranger wearing my skin.

There are blood vessels streaked throughout the whites of my eyes. I look like a monster. An imposter is taking residence in my body.

My eyes move down to the bruises wrapped around my neck. I slowly reach up and touch my neck.

Gently so as to not scare myself.

My hand lingers there.

I take a deep breath, yet don't make any attempt to move away from the mirror. I am glued to the floor. I have to face this. I can't brush it off as if it didn't happen.

I witness the rise and fall of my chest as I breathe slowly in and out. Without breaking eye contact with myself, tears start to fall.

Not hysterically, just plainly.

More matter-of-fact than emotional.

I don't sob.

I watch the tears smear my face and I don't try to wipe them away.

They are allowed to be there. At this moment, I fear if I reject this experience, I may never cry again.

So, I lean closer to myself.

I search for the girl I once was, frozen in photographs scattered across my life – smiling, laughing, carefree.

I see myself as a child running through the backyard of my childhood home, our dog chasing at my heels. I see my father pushing me on the swing, my laughter spilling into the air. I see teenage me in high school, sitting with friends, gossiping about boys and futures that felt promising.

She is not the one staring back at me now.

Suddenly I have to blink.

I force myself to stay present.

It's three in the morning and I can't sleep because I am riddled with nightmares.

So, face them, I tell myself.

There is nothing you can do to change what happened a little over a week ago, but you can try to find some kind of resemblance of healing. Even if it's only one step.

Don't be scared, I tell the girl in the mirror, without moving my lips.

Be brave, I whisper silently, as my hand moves down towards my chest.

I hesitate briefly and then I slip my robe open, letting it slide to the side to expose my nude breast.

Recognition flickers, just a little.

There's no bruising there, so it feels more like I am looking at the girl I once knew.

Another breath.

Another blink.

The tears have subsided.

The pain in my eyes remains though.

They lack that light we have when something makes us happy.

I am twenty-three years old, yet the woman in the mirror has aged by a decade. The woman in the mirror doesn't know yet what that means.

I wrap my robe around myself again and walk back to bed, knowing the moment has loosened its grip. I feel slightly steadier.

There was a small glimmer in those eyes — just enough to hold onto. I slide beneath the covers, close my eyes and fall back into a restless sleep.

My final thought before drifting off is simple: I am not the girl I once was. But someday I will be better.

I promise myself. Someday.

CHAPTER 46

Grocery Store

It was just like any other day. Late August. The kind of day where the heat lingers even inside air-conditioned buildings.

Although not known for it being extremely warm here in The Pacific Northwest, this seemed like an unusually warm summer with less rainfall than normal.

I walked into the grocery store with a list in my head. Or maybe it was on a scrap of paper. I can't remember. My mind was a crowded place back then.

As I moved through the automatic doors, the blast of cool air hit my face and for a moment I just stood there, watching people go about their normal lives. There were the sounds of grocery carts rolling and cashiers chatting lively to customers as they were scanning their items.

I heard a baby crying somewhere nearby and it felt as if ordinary life was happening at full volume while mine felt muted and far away.

A strange dread simmered in my stomach. There was no clear reason for me to feel this way. Just a heaviness that followed me down every aisle. I kept moving. Slow but determined, like if I stopped too long I might not start again.

Someone brushed against my arm in the narrow aisle and I held my breath momentarily at the uninvited touch.

My breath caught in my throat, my body reacting before my brain could reason with it.

I said nothing. Just kept walking.

The produce section glowed under a water mist and bright lights.

Rows of fresh green beans, neat piles of corn, bright red strawberries and bananas hanging in perfect yellow arcs. It should have felt comforting and familiar but instead it felt like too many decisions.

There had been so many decisions that had needed to be made recently; this one simply felt more daunting than all the others.

Maybe apples.

What kind?

Fuji?

Granny Smith?

Why were there so many choices for something so simple? I placed a bunch of half-green bananas in my cart. You always buy them a little green or they go bad too fast I thought to myself. Some part of me still knew how to plan for tomorrow, even if I couldn't picture next week.

By the time I reached the meat section, I convinced myself I would make my family spaghetti recipe. One of the few meals I could make without thinking. Then I considered making a shrimp fettuccine with a heavy garlic and parmesan cream sauce.

Maybe even a Caesar salad with avocado in the dressing like I once had at a friend's house. That felt fancy. An attempt at some normalcy.

But my legs wouldn't move and the cart handle felt heavy under my hands. My chest felt tight. The idea of choosing ingredients, of cooking, of feeding myself – it all felt impossible and not something I could do at that moment in time.

Maybe tomorrow I could; just not today.

Frankly sitting in my car and crying for an hour sounded far more manageable.

My heart was so sad that day. Not for one single reason, but for a thousand quiet ones. August has always been a loaded month. It still is to this day.

If you've ever lost someone in your life, you are part of the club; none of us yet but all of us will eventually become members of; the *"death anniversary club."*

My mother died in August when I was just a month and three days old. And two months earlier, my husband had tried to kill me.

Now he sat in county jail while I sorted through the wreckage he left behind. How was that fair? He had three meals handed to him.

A bed. A schedule.

I had bills, decisions, memories, and silence.

He didn't have to stand in a grocery aisle wondering what kind of apples to buy or whether he might abandon a half-filled cart to cry in the parking lot.

And, he didn't have a mother's death anniversary coming around the corner.

Perhaps, that day, it all was just too much.

I was tired in a way sleep doesn't fix and lost in a way naps don't solve.

I know we are all familiar with how people talk about *"bouncing back,"* but there was no life to bounce back to for me.

The life I had was gone. Shattered as if I had just dropped an egg in the dairy aisle. It would take time, probably more than I cared to admit, but I need to learn how to land somewhere new.

So, I went to the grocery store.

And all I bought were green bananas.

A small victory, but a victory all the same.

CHAPTER 47

Strength

When people ask me how I was able to escape, I loosely use the word *strength*. It's the easiest answer.

The cleanest one. The one that fits neatly into conversation without making people too uncomfortable.

But what determines a person's strength? Is it physical? Is it mental? Is it both braided together so tightly you can't tell where one ends and the other begins?

From the outside looking in, most would assume my mental state during those years was fragile. Weak. Broken down.

After almost six years with a man who chipped away at me, isolated me from friends and family – though never completely – surely, I had been reduced to something small.

But that isn't entirely true.

In the beginning, the manipulation came on quietly. Faster than I remember, if I'm honest. I had blinders on. Like a horse fitted with leather patches that block peripheral vision. That was me – seeing only what was directly in front of me, not what was circling from the sides.

I was out in the pasture, yes – but not grazing peacefully. I was trying to figure out how to get home. Where *was* home?

Where was the place I belonged? Where was my stall and my bale of hay?

As the years passed, something shifted. I began to remember who I was. I was outgoing. Friendly. I could talk to anyone.

I was a professional wedding photographer, for God's sake – commanding a room full of nervous bridesmaids and distracted groomsmen without flinching. I directed entire wedding parties with confidence. I made people laugh. I knew my craft, and I was good at it.

I was never shy. I was never afraid of my own voice. But this is where manipulation does its most cruel work. Not by destroying you overnight – but by planting seeds.

"You are so stupid. Why can't you just cook dinner?"

"What is wrong with you? This house is a mess."

"Oh baby, you're beautiful—but if you lost five pounds, you could be a Playboy Bunny. Just for me."

"Why did you cut your hair? You look fucking ugly. You look like a boy."

"I love you more than anyone ever will."

"If I can't have you, I don't want to live anymore."

"Why is the laundry room such a disaster? You're a terrible housewife!"

When the person who promised to protect you says these things often enough, parts of you begin to believe them.

Not all at once.

Just small splinters.

They slip into your internal dialogue and start echoing back at you.

But here's the truth: somewhere underneath it all, I knew better.

That's why I asked for the divorce.

I was the one who said, *"Enough."*

You don't get to speak to me like that. You don't get to shrink me.

What I didn't understand was that leaving required strategy.

It never occurred to me I would be in danger by simply leaving our marriage.

Turns out this is the time when most women are the most vulnerable. Please, if you don't take anything else away from this book, remember this part. I wish I had known. But now, you my dear reader, know.

Tuck it in the back of your mind somewhere, should you ever need it.

When a woman asserts her own power and control by leaving, she is the most exposed. It's the time when men feel the most threatened and some will do everything in their power to change the outcome.

I didn't know what he was capable of. I didn't know that ending it would ignite something darker.

Strength comes in many forms. Most of us don't know we possess it until the moment we're forced to reach for it.

It's in the bad news. The loss. The diagnosis.

It's in the betrayal. The moment life explodes into something unrecognizable.

Or the moment you find yourself staring down the barrel of a shotgun held by your estranged husband.

That's when the mirror appears.

Just for a second.

And you see yourself clearly.

Before all of this, I was an avid rollerblader. Three to five mornings a week, I met friends at a designated spot along the bike trail. We laced up and went. The first stretch was downhill – fast, exhilarating.

Which meant the return was brutal.

Three or four miles out. Three or four miles back. Eight miles total of burning thighs and screaming lungs. Sprinting the last stretch. Collapsing into the grass.

Gasping for air.

Smiling at the sky.

I was five foot ten and somewhere between 135 and 145 pounds, depending on the week. Lean. Strong. Full of spit and vinegar. My legs were powerful. My lungs were trained.

My body knew how to endure discomfort.

So, was that it?

Was it my physical strength that saved me?

Was I fit enough that he couldn't overpower me? Was he too weak to finish what he started?

He wasn't a tall man. He claimed to be five foot nine. Reality was closer to five seven or five eight. I vaguely remember a slight heel in his wedding shoes. But that doesn't matter.

He was fit enough. Strong enough. So why am I still here?

At one point, when I was lying face down on the concrete outside our front door. That space when I smelled oil and gasoline, remember? I took a deep breath – probably a mistake.

And just before everything started to fade, there was a split-second thought. Not a conversation. Not a prayer. Just a flash.

You are strong enough.

That wasn't about my biceps. It wasn't about my thighs or my lungs.

It was about my mind.

The strength that saved me didn't come from muscle memory.

It came from knowing instinctually what he needed me to say and taking advantage of his weakness - despite the chaos, my mind supplied the words necessary to feed his ego. He believed me because he wanted to believe me.

The ultimate lies I fed him – the words he wanted – became my key to the front door. It's how I finally broke open the front door.

And I ran. That was strength.

Strength isn't just a fit body. It's the ability to think when terror tries to shut your brain down.

It's outmaneuvering your monster.

It's the decision – made in milliseconds – that you will NOT die today.

Strength finds you when you need it most.

It doesn't always roar.

Sometimes it whispers.

Sometimes it lies convincingly.

Sometimes it runs.

It found my heart when it was breaking. It steadied my breath when it was shallow. It carried my legs when they wanted to collapse.

Strength saved me that day.

Not just the kind you can see – but the kind that lives quietly in the mind, waiting for the moment it's called forward.

When it was called, it showed up.

And guess what? The will to live is the ultimate strength.

CHAPTER 48

Because You Loved Me

Afterwards, I wanted to believe you loved me. Or at least that you had loved me once.

I wanted to believe the blood smeared across my face was because you loved me. I wanted to believe the nervous knots twisting inside my stomach were because you loved me.

My hair, tangled and gritty with dried blood, was because you said you loved me. The bruises around my neck. The burst blood vessels in the whites of my eyes as I stared blankly at my reflection — all of it because you loved me.

How ridiculous does that sound?

The moment those thoughts entered my mind, they dissolved just as quickly. Ours wasn't love.

You didn't love me.

I simply wanted it to be love.

I was wrong. So very wrong.

The day I walked down the aisle on my brother's arm, I believed I was walking toward love. Never in a million years did I imagine it was anything else.

Yet you proved me wrong.

In more ways than I could have imagined.

I never believed I was being abused or manipulated. Me? Never.

I may have been young, but I wasn't blind. I saw your strengths and your flaws. I saw a man I promised to stand beside in sickness and health… until death do us part.

I just never imagined you would try to take that vow literally. That you would try to kill me when I stopped loving you. Because you could no longer control me. Because at last, I saw you for who you truly were. And what I saw was not a man in love.

Maybe it was always about control.

No… there is no *"maybe."*

It was always about control. Control over everything. Control over everyone. And if you didn't get your way, there were consequences.

I am more guarded now. Trust doesn't come easily. Not in ways that matter. Not in the fragile places relationships require. I hate admitting that, but this story isn't meant to sound pretty.

It is meant to be honest.

For a long time, I believed you took from me the ability to believe I could be loved by a partner.

In relationships afterward, I tried too hard. Or I ended things too early — before I could be hurt again. I wanted to control when things ended.

Because you loved me.

Because you loved me so much you couldn't bear the thought of me leaving. This is not love. It never was.

Love is more than vows spoken in front of 150 guests. Love is more than a tuxedo and a wedding dress. Love is more than words spoken during a ceremony. Love is the quiet promise made when no one is watching. Love is a silent glance across a crowded room.

Love is coffee brewing in the kitchen before the other person wakes. Love is peace. Love is safety. Love is freedom, not fear. Love is never manipulation. Love is never threats. Love cannot be forced.

Love is certainly not the inheritance you violently drained from my bank account. Because you never loved me.

And, in hindsight, I never truly loved you either. I was in love with the idea of you. And we both know how that turned out.

The idea of the person you were was never seated in reality.

You pursued me because of money. Not love. You pursued me so you could take control of the narrative of my life all to benefit your life. Again not love. None of this happened because you loved me.

And, maybe that is the most terrifying thing of all.

CHAPTER 49

Why Can't She Just Love Me?

"I'm sitting on top of her, pinning her down so she can't move. I just need her to stop fighting, to stop trying to get away.

That's when I see it.

The telephone wire she carefully ran along the trim leading into her office.

She has no idea how hard any of this really is. She thinks she built this business on her own. She doesn't see everything I've done to hold it together. There is no way she would be where she is right now if I wasn't here doing the hard work.

I don't understand why she can't see that she needs me.

The wire feels cold in my hands as I wrap it around her neck. This will work.

There is no way she can leave me now.

I don't feel good. Damn, my hands are slipping. I pull tighter.

Soon she is still beneath the weight of my body. There you go, baby. Just calm down.

Before I understand what's happening, she is up – ripping the wire from my hands and from her neck. I fall backward onto the floor. But I can't stop. She's mine."

The woman I am today sits in her home office nearly thirty years later, trying to analyze his mind.

"Are these the thoughts that went through his head that day?" I ask out loud.

Even now, in safety far removed from that morning, it feels intrusive to pull on this thread. Yet powerful. There's an unease rising inside me, placing me right back under his watchful eyes. There is power in discovery, though. In trying to understand the mind that tried to silence me.

"Get back here. Stop trying to leave our house. I'm running after her now. I trap her in the kitchen. Good. She's still here. Wait – what? She stabbed me in the neck with one of our kitchen knives. I'm okay though, baby. I forgive you.
I can't think straight. I can't breathe.

Don't you understand? This is still our home. We belong together. I forgive you for hurting me this way. I just need you to see this is because I love you. Please. Just let me hold you. You can't leave me Hjordis. You are mine!"

Of course, all of this is conjecture.

I have no idea what thoughts went through his mind that morning as I tried to defend myself from his attempt to kill me. But I lean in because of something he *actually* said before I made it out the front door:

"We just need to take a shower and wash all this blood off of us…"

It suggests that in his mind, he had done nothing wrong.

Not really. It suggests this was all my fault.

Which aligns with his defense attorney's questions:

"Did he use all his strength when he pulled the telephone wire around your neck? Did he use all his strength when he hit you in the head with the baseball bat?"

They say time brings wisdom.

I can't be certain, but I believe he never took accountability. Behind rose-colored glasses, he did not see this for what it was – and likely never would.

Perhaps he couldn't.

Or perhaps he was that delusional.

He was not in the same experience as I was. He saw this as love. Proof that he would fight this hard. That his love was real. Pure. Everlasting.

He would do anything not to lose it. Even if that meant killing me.

Two people can live in the same moment and experience entirely different realities. I can say he hit me in the head with a baseball bat intending to shatter my skull. He could say his hands slipped and it barely grazed me as he leaned over to set it down.

Sometimes two things can be true.

But not here.

Take two brothers. One remembers their father at every baseball game. The other remembers him absent. Both experiences may be true.

One may have been too focused on his swing to notice his father in the stands.

Perspective.

But attempted murder is not perspective.

There is such a thing as selfish love.

The kind we want because we want it. Because we believe we deserve it. Was it that? Or was it something darker?

Could it be what he said out loud that morning – that I was going to die? That if he couldn't have me, no one could?

The wiser version of me believes so.

It wasn't love for me. It was love for himself. He could not allow me to leave because that would fracture the image he had of himself.

"It's better she dies than ruin my life."

CHAPTER 50

Am From The Land Of The Midnight Sun

I had many ideas for what to name this book. Choosing one has not been easy. I am not an author – not yet, at least – and I suspect the title may change before this story is finished. But no matter what it is called, it will always be about finding the front door.

Because beyond that door is where my life continues to move, shift, and survive.

I am more than the young woman who found herself trapped in violence and fear, uncertain of what would come next. Where I came from was always bigger than that morning. Where I came from quietly gave me the strength to find that front door.

I am from the land of the midnight sun, from Viking blood and people who carry emotion behind steady faces.

I am from homemade *"Norwegian"* spaghetti with peas and *"hot-dogs"* stirred in, from cornflakes sprinkled with sugar and just a few splashes of milk.

I am from the tears and fears of a father grieving the loss of his wife and my mother. I am the baby who never attended her funeral.

I am from snow and ice, and summers spent digging in warm sand, burying Marie crackers like treasure.

I am from the moment I birthed my children, nursing them while singing "Amazing Graze" in the dark, later watching them sleep stretched across their beds as young teenagers.

I am from once being a girl in a woman's body, feeling the soft silk of a nightgown, and from trembling awake after nightmares I could not name.

I am from pizza baked on homemade crust rolled out by my sister, and from being paid for babysitting with a carton of cigarettes from my brother.

I am from going downhill skiing while my big brother follows behind to keep me safe.

I am from late nights listening to the slow drip of a coffee pot filling, counting seconds like they mattered. I am from vodka brewed in a basement from potatoes grown in our yard, and later from buying it under fluorescent lights at my local grocery store.

I am from growing up motherless and pouring everything I have into becoming a mother myself.

I am built from fear and truth, from loss and survival.

I am from ruins and ashes.

And I am still here. I am more than the circumstances of my life. I am the sum of what comes after.

I am not perfect as perfection is a myth. Yet, I am perfectly imperfect. In fact, that is one of several tattoos I have adorned on my body.

That said, I like who I became – especially the woman who stepped through that front door.

CHAPTER 51

It's As If He Died Too

After the smoke cleared, it was almost as if my husband – although not in the true sense of the word anymore – had also died. He had suddenly been added to the list of people who had left me.

By dying. Although he was very much alive. Simply not alive to me, because he would never again be part of my life.

So, he died.

Like my mother.

My father.

My beloved dog, Tell.

Even my guinea pig, Suzie, who lived five long and beautiful years for such a small creature.

So again, another death. It felt like a similar loss, yet completely different.

Was I sad in the same way my world went up in smoke when I was twelve and my father unexpectedly died? Would this bring sorrow for years to come? Would I still long for this person I had once loved?

The answers were not immediate. I couldn't explain them quickly, or in any language that would make sense. I couldn't even describe them in my own silent thoughts.

It would take years to understand the depth of his actions and how they spun my world sideways. Not always sideways, but enough that memories of what happened would swoop in, paralyze me, and then disappear just as quickly – leaving me breathless, aching, fragile, small.

You may ask why I would mourn him. I wasn't mourning him. I was mourning the me I was before.

I was mourning the loss of the naïve belief that people do not do these things to one another. I was mourning the idea that life could be expected and simple and beautiful and kind.

I have first-hand knowledge of what it feels like to be an orphan. To live without the two people who gave me life. It does not matter how many years pass; it becomes part of you.

An invisible thread woven through the tangible fabric of daily living. It shifts over time – sometimes heavy, sometimes quiet – but it never leaves. It is both loss and momentum.

It sits on my shoulder, in my chest, within my breath.

It is part of my story.

I have no idea what it is like to be a widow. I cannot call myself one, yet it feels as if there are similarities. One day you are living your life – uncertain, but moving forward – and the next, everything changes without warning. No further contact.

Only courtrooms and paperwork, which now feel surreal in memory. And when that finally ends, the realization arrives: you will never see this man again.

He is dead to you.

As a widow, I imagine I would cry silently into a pillow some nights. I did that. I imagine I would remember the good moments and cling to them, because they are easier to hold than reality.

I did that too.

I imagine I would miss his voice, his laugh, his tenderness – because that would mean it wasn't all a lie. I did that.

I imagine I would want to scream at him, to finish the last argument, to believe there was still something left to say.

I did that too. I wanted him to tell me he was sorry. I wanted him to tell me why.

When someone dies, they remain exactly as you last saw them. They do not age. For me, I know he has aged. He has lived a life. He did not die. Yet the loss remains and collides with every rational thought.

Perhaps because grief and loss and pain do not come from rational places.

None of this is rational.

The questions remain unanswered.

Just like when my father died. So many questions. So many desires to know my father as a person instead of the limited version a child sees.

This is not the same loss – but it is close enough to echo the same questions.

So, although he did not die that morning, set in motion by his own actions, it felt as if he had.

A part of me prayed that first night he would die from his self-inflicted gunshot wound.

Somehow, that was not part of the story.

Some days I wonder… had he died, would I be writing this book?

CHAPTER 52

Alford Plea

There are moments when the legal system fails you. Probably for people on both sides of the law. But when someone is given the opportunity to step away from something they so clearly did, the system itself feels broken.

I knew I could have pushed for a jury trial. I could have fought harder. But there also comes a point when you simply want the nightmare you are living – wide awake – to end.

That is how an Alford plea enters your life. He would not admit wrongdoing.

He would never admit that he had gone there that day with one intent and one intent only and that was to murder me.

The original charges of Attempted Murder in the First Degree and Unlawful Imprisonment would be reduced.

Reduced to what exactly? I could look it up in court documents, but I chose not to. The legal phrasing feels hollow. It doesn't reflect what happened. It simply means he accepted a deal because he and his legal team believed a jury trial would end worse for him.

The judge would decide his sentence. There was the possibility of what is called an exceptional sentence – up to ten years.

After countless letters written to the court by my family and friends, and after I gave my own statement while he stood less than ten feet away from me, the judge sentenced my estranged husband to 7.7666 years in prison.

The precision of that number felt surreal.

As if trauma could be measured in decimals.

The air in the courtroom felt sharp and heavy. I noticed his parents sitting behind him, along with his longtime employer and his wife. They were there to support him. I remember glancing at them briefly and shaking my head.

To them, he was still their son. Their employee. Their person. Nothing had changed except that he was about to spend years in prison and would leave as a convicted felon, stripped of rights like voting or carrying a firearm.

What seemed invisible that day was the girl who had once been welcomed into their lives – now quietly pushed out because of what he had done to her.

I didn't look at him. Not really. I could feel his presence beside me, separated by two attorneys, and that alone made my knees unsteady.

The day I walked out the front door months earlier, I knew I never wanted to see him again. There was nothing left to say. And, simultaneously, there was so much to say. Impossible conversation not worth pursuing nor would it be allowed with the no contact order in effect.

There was so much I would never understand. What he had done - crossed a line that cannot be walked back.

I do not remember hearing him speak that day. I do not remember if he showed remorse. My mind may have blocked it out, or perhaps there simply was none to witness.

I spoke; reading from a prepared statement. Most of it is a blur in my mind today. But, I did speak. He couldn't keep me silent anymore. I also wrote a four page, single space letter to the Judge, which read in part;

"I never thought that I would become part of a statistic, but I have. I have now become part of the large number of women who are battered. However, if you look at me, you do not see your typical battered woman. I am strong, both emotionally and physically, and I suppose that strength was instilled in me from the very beginning, from my father and my family. Before my father passed away, he loved to tell me how he knocked on the glass of the incubator that I was in due to having been born three months premature, and since the doctors thought I would die, my father knocked on that glass and said, 'You are going to make it. You are strong and a fighter and you are

going to live.' Those words were ringing in my ears during this brutal struggle with my estranged husband, when he tried to end my life. I am lucky not to have become part of the statistics of dead women at the hands of their spouses."

I remember realizing that some people are capable of extraordinary harm while still believing they are justified. That realization is its own kind of horror.

Many letters written by family and friends were sent to the judge urging sentencing to be at the highest range allowed by law. Their words helped carry me through a moment when I felt the system could not. When institutions fracture, community often holds the pieces together.

My village showed up for me when I needed it most.

"For six years, Hjordis had her self-confidence chipped away little by little until finally she knew she had to get away. We are very proud of her courage to face him and stop the abuse. His actions in response to her decision to leave him, have shaken us. He committed a crime not just against Hjordis but against all those he knew. For this he deserves Just punishment." wrote one friend in a letter to the Judge.

"During a visit at the end of May, I noticed a marked change in my friend. She was very discouraged. During the first part of June she told me of her request for the two of them to seek marriage counseling and of his refusal. When I saw her four days (after the attack), and the remaining bruises, stitches, cuts, abrasions on her body, I was amazed she had survived. Most of the physical wounds have healed (now), but the psychological and spiritual wounds have not. These wounds will take many years to heal" wrote another.

Court records will never tell the full story. It cannot hold fear, or pain, or survival. It only records outcomes.

"Her husband was extremely controlling and exhibited strange behavior the entire two years I've been acquainted with him. For example, he bought things compulsively until the house was filled to overflowing with stuff and he continued buying until he'd also filled three commercial storage areas. He constantly told Hjordis she was dumb and not capable of running her photography business, and claimed he knew more because he had a business degree (turns out he did not)." states another friend.

"We had very little contact over a period of four years, due to my dislike of him and the fact he did not want Hjordis to be in touch with me. This shows how from the start of their relationship, he wanted total control over her." my sister wrote.

"I want that man behind bars as long as possible, because he has ruined my little sister's life. These horrible things will follow her for the rest of her life. I can only hope that she will be able to have a real life again, without nightmares." my oldest brother wrote.

Reading their words now, I am reminded how visible my pain was to everyone but me. No matter how we think we are keeping things private, people can ultimately see what is happening to you, even if you don't.

At least he received prison time.

At least there was acknowledgment – even if incomplete.

I sometimes wonder how the case would unfold if it happened today. But this story belongs to then, not now.

Walking out of that courtroom, I felt finished.

Exhausted.

Older than I had been six months earlier.

Yet strangely steady.

I also felt a sense of protection from my family and friends wrapping me up, urging me forward.

I was wearing a light beige business suit, and I remember thinking I looked stronger than I felt. I can still hear the sound of my heels striking the courthouse floor with each step toward the exit.

Alford plea or not, I know what he did.

And so does he.

When the courthouse door closed behind me, it felt like the first time I could finally turn toward my future.

CHAPTER 53

Afraid Of The Dark?

It was the middle of the night, and there wasn't a light anywhere in the house. I stumbled out of bed and reached for the switch.

Nothing. I flipped it again. Still nothing.

I made my way towards my bathroom in the dark. My hand fumbled along the wall until I found the bathroom switch. Relief washed over me. This light must work. I flipped it up.

Nothing. Again. And again. And again.

Only darkness. Wait. What was that? Who's there?

I sensed movement in my bedroom yet I live alone. No one should be here. It was 2:48 a.m.

I stepped back toward the bedroom, trying to see through the darkness, and before I could react, he was standing in front of me.

He reached out quickly, his lips not moving to speak. He wrapped his hands around my neck, and squeezed. It was slow at first, his dark eyes locked into mine, only inches away. He grinned at me. Then he squeezed harder.

Suddenly there was nothing.

No light and no pulse.

He came back to finish the job.

"Mom! Mom, wake up! We're going to be late for school!"

My eyes flew open and for a brief moment, I didn't know where I was. Then I did. I push the covers away and swing my legs over the side of my bed. It was a dream.

Not all of it – but the darkness, the light switch, and him returning…that was the dream. I quickly threw myself into some sweats, shoved my long hair into a hair clip, and rushed to the bathroom. Cold water splashed against my face, grounding me, if only briefly.

The kids bustled through the house. I poured cereal and milk, reheated yesterday's coffee, and before long, we were heading out the door. The kids chatted in the car, but their voices sounded muffled as my mind raced. Why that dream? Why now?

After dropping them off at school, I return home. I need fresh coffee and a hot shower.

That is the part of this life that still catches me off guard. When I least expect it, it returns – in my sleep. And the truth is, the notion of not having lights on in my house is ridiculous. There is always a light – sometimes five – glowing somewhere.

I don't walk into darkness willingly anymore. Because things hide in the shadows . In the space between light and dark, that is where evil feels all too familiar.

But the truth is, he didn't hide in the shadows.

He walked straight into the house that morning. I let him in because I never imagined I was in danger. Things were bad between us and I was moving out that day. But never once did I think, "*He is going to try to kill me.*"

Maybe that is why, in the years since, I keep the lights on. Because light lets you see what stands in front of you. It isn't that I am afraid of the dark.

I fought darkness once. If I had to, I would fight it again. The light means more than illumination.

When we face darkness, we can fall so deeply it feels impossible to find our way back.

When everything feels broken and we begin to believe the world – and the people we love – would be better off without us.

I have walked that road.

"Are you a danger to yourself or anyone else?"

"No, I am not."

"I'll speak to the nurse about getting you released."

"Thank you... could I have my phone to call for a ride?"

"Of course. Just hang tight a few minutes longer, dear."

It is a lonely road.

Suicide is often labeled selfish. How could someone do that to their children? Their family? Their friends?

But when someone falls that low, they often believe they are doing everyone a favor. Removing themselves so no one has to carry the weight of them.

That belief is not true.

Too many choose a permanent solution for a temporary problem. After darkness comes light.

Sometimes only a sliver.

Just enough to see what darkness hides – the things people bury inside themselves because they never flip the switch.

That is the darkness I fear.

The switch that refuses to respond no matter how many times you flip it. Up and down. Up and down.

That is why every room in my home has a light. Just a little one. Since I pay the electric bill, the lights will stay on. So I can always see what stands in front of me.

CHAPTER 54

Time Doesn't Stand Still

Maybe everything in life happens at the moment it is meant to.

That sounds comforting in theory.

When I saw him again, it felt like anything but comfort. I don't even know how to describe what I felt in that instant. Only that it was nothing like what I expected.

He looked ordinary. Not dangerous. Not monstrous. Just… a regular man. The kind you pass in a grocery store without a second glance. The kind you might trust to hold a door open or coach your kid's basketball team. I almost didn't recognize him at all.

When his profile photo first appeared on my screen, I was seconds away from scrolling past. Then recognition slammed into me. I gasped out loud.

"It can't be… Shit.
That's the motherfucker who tried to kill me."

It started the way many things do now – falling into an internet rabbit hole during a break at work, one of those moments where a phone becomes both a distraction and doorway.

I discovered his father had died in 2018. The online obituary included photos. One of them stopped me cold. It was a portrait I had taken years earlier at his parents' fiftieth wedding anniversary. Professionally, I can admit it was a beautiful photograph. The lighting was soft, their expressions warm, carefully framed the way I had been trained to capture a portrait that would stand the test of time.

I couldn't help wondering if anyone had ever questioned it. Did anyone ever ask who took that photograph? Did anyone consider replacing it, knowing their former daughter-in-law had nearly been murdered by their son? Or was it easier to leave the past undisturbed, safely compartmentalized into silence?

After all, his family didn't try to kill me. He did. Funny thing; loyalty rarely asks for an explanation. They were not there when he told me I was going to die.

They didn't hear him say, *"Since you miss your parents so much, today you're going to meet them again."*

The man in the profile picture looked worn. He had aged of course, and his hair had turned solid gray. His smile was crooked, eyes hidden behind mirrored sunglasses. He looked like someone's neighbor. Someone who drinks black coffee every morning before heading to work. Someone who gives motivational speeches to teenagers before games. Just a regular sixty-something year old man with a receding hairline going about his life as if he did nothing wrong.

I tucked my phone back into my pants pocket as I returned to work and simply shook my head at the fact I had in fact located an image of him online. Later, alone with my thoughts, I opened the photos again. I tilted my phone, squinted, zoomed in, searching for proof that I was mistaken. I wasn't.

For me, he had been frozen in time. For decades he had been preserved as the man who attacked me, who spoke in threats, whose face hovered inches from mine while I fought to breathe. Intellectually, I knew he must have aged. Emotionally, I was unprepared for the reality of it. My body reacted before my mind could catch up and pain spread throughout my chest. It was a physical and emotional pain I couldn't ignore.

For a moment, I wanted to undo everything. To rewind my life and step out of this reality entirely. The weight of it felt unbearable, as though it had always been unbearable and I had simply learned to carry it without noticing. I had unknowingly carried all of it within me – leaving me no room for healing and emotional growth as I too aged.

Suddenly I was back on 73rd Street, fighting for my life. More real now than it was then, because suddenly there's an understanding of the evil that existed within the walls of that house.

Time has a cruel way of sharpening memory. The realization came next – quiet and horrifying.

I might not recognize him if we crossed paths today. He does not look like the man I married when I was nineteen years old. Yet part of me had unconsciously expected time to preserve him exactly as he existed in my mind's eye. Maybe that was never ignorance. Maybe it was survival. I am not the same woman I was some almost thirty years ago, yet I expected him to look the same? I had actually expected to be able to recognize him out in the world yet now I wasn't so sure I could.

In the photograph, he appears harmless. The sunglasses hide his eyes, but I know what lives behind them. I know what he is capable of. And I cannot help wondering whether he stopped. Whether he learned anything in prison.

Whether another woman ever stood where I once stood, trying to leave, searching desperately for a way out.

Did he stop manipulating women into thinking he was the only one who could love them? Did he continue to fool people into thinking he was charming and funny even though a bit reserved at times?

He rebuilt his life.

He remarried and became a father to a son. He exists inside a version of normal that seems almost impossible to reconcile with the man who once tried to end my life.

The version of him I knew didn't track with how his life ended up looking like.

I did not once think he would father a child as I would recognize much later, him putting me off to have babies *"some day"* was his way of saying, he never wanted to have any.

I rebuilt mine too – filled with love, joy, children, and accomplishments that stretch far beyond this darkness. Those memories are mine. Completely mine. I survived. I won.

Still, part of me resents that time moved forward for him. That he was granted years he once tried to steal from me in seventy-five violent minutes. Minutes in which he never hesitated, never blinked nor paused to question his own actions.

I always feared he would hurt someone else. That another woman might not find the front door in time.

Because the truth is, he does not look like a monster.

He looks like a regular man.

And that is the most terrifying part of all.

CHAPTER 55

Going Back To The House

It was a regular Thursday when I decided to face something I had spent years avoiding.

Trauma has a quiet persistence. You can bury it beneath busy years, beneath children and businesses and marriages and rebuilding, but it waits patiently.

Life is curious in this way.

How it chooses the right time for you to lean into your pain.

It's so easy to just keep ignoring the pull.

And sometimes life chooses the moment when you are finally strong enough to turn around and look at it.

I do not regret the twenty-five years that came after him. I raised my children, built businesses, and created a home filled with safety and love. My second marriage ended, but it gave me a life I am deeply proud of — one shaped by resilience rather than fear.

Now that my children are grown, silence has given memory more room to speak. The question was never whether I needed to confront it, only how to do so without unraveling myself completely. I am painfully aware that I need to process all of this in a way that I don't bring more harm to myself.

That Thursday, after finishing with a client who happened to live in the town where I once lived, I turned right instead of left toward home. I didn't have a plan beyond that.

I stopped at the light leading to the street where the house still stands. My heart pounded against my ribs as if it were trying to escape my chest. My hands trembled on the steering wheel. The red arrow felt suspended in time.

I turned off the podcast playing through my speakers and reached for music, then stopped. Silence felt necessary. If I was going to face this, I needed to hear everything — every memory, every thought, every emotion clawing its way forward. I needed to be present for all of it. At last, the light turned green and I pushed down on the gas pedal, moving my SUV through the intersection.

I passed the old fire station, the library, and noticed a new firehouse standing nearby. I wondered, briefly, if any of the EMTs who responded to the 911 call all those years ago were still working there.

The trees lining the road had grown taller. Their leaves glowed in the afternoon sun as warm air drifted through my open window. For a fleeting moment, nature wrapped itself around me like a soft blanket. The sky blue, the air warm as it spilled in my driver side window. The sun was as bright as ever. Giving me the light I yearned for and not darkness as I traveled down this old familiar road — as if reminding me I was traveling toward memory, not back into darkness.

I passed the apartment complex where I once lived with my family. Passed streets that once held friendships now long gone. Just around the next bend and I would be back. Back to the place that almost broke me and nearly ended my life.

I pull over and park across the street from the house. Trembling as my eyes scan the house and property. I sat there, sinking in the driver seat as if to disappear completely within it.

I sat much longer than I expected, gathering breath I wasn't sure I had. Finally, I get out of the car, keys and cell phone in hand. After several cars pass, I run across the street – the same street I had run into years earlier after escaping.

The same street where a car slowed, looked at a half-naked, bleeding twenty-three-year-old woman standing in the road… and drove away.

My feet touched pavement that felt both foreign and painfully familiar. The past rose around me like a world I had once escaped but never fully left behind.

Labels like "victim" and "survivor" hovered at the edges of my thoughts. I have never liked either, though if forced to choose, survivor is the only reason these words exist.

I walked toward the house.

It became difficult to breathe, yet I kept going.

The lawn looked much the same — uneven grass dotted with dandelions. I remembered sitting there years ago, taking photographs with my German Shepherd, Vinnie. He could not save me that day, though I know he would have tried.

A red car sat in the driveway.

I hesitated before climbing the concrete steps and knocking on the door. When my knuckle connected with the surface, I realized it was the same door I had fought to open.

It was just painted over.

Nobody came to the door, so I slowly backed away.

As I stepped backward, I noticed changes.

The bottom step had been filled in with fresh concrete. The odd hole beside the stairs was gone, replaced by a smooth walkway leading toward the backyard. The realization hit me without warning.

The place where he forced my face into the asphalt no longer existed. I shouldn't have been surprised. In some ways, it felt right. That exact space, that precise moment of violence, had been buried beneath something new.

Standing there, fully grown, I was suddenly transported back inside the house. His hands closed around my throat again.

I felt the panic, the frantic scratching at his fingers, the terrifying clarity that if he held on for another minute or two, I would die.

That memory has never faded. It is sobering to know that a mere couple of minutes exist between living and dying.

Yet here I stood — alive, shaking, but safe — twenty-five years later.

I studied the house one last time.

The pastel green paint had been replaced with pale yellow. The wood trim around the garage sagged with age. Small, ordinary signs of time passing.

It wasn't until I sat back inside my car that the full force of memory hit me. I didn't know I could still have a physical reaction to the memory of that day, all these years later. My heart felt like it was breaking all over again for that innocent girl. I realized trauma does not disappear simply because life continues.

It waits quietly in the body, patient as stone.

It took several minutes before I could start the engine.

At forty-eight years old, I momentarily forgot how to drive.

People say to lean into the memory of your trauma, so you can hold it, spit at it, yell and cry in order to release it all.

For years, I believed I already had.

Sitting there, I understood how wrong I had been. I felt heartbreak for the twenty-three-year-old woman who believed she was fine. I felt frustration toward my present self for believing healing was something that could be rushed or postponed.

I called a friend to help calm my frazzled nerves. I had convinced myself I could do this alone — a habit formed from years of self-reliance. I was wrong. Her calm voice grounded me enough to pull away from the curb and begin driving home.

I layered myself in emotional armor as I drove, determined to return to the life I built — to my children, my home, my carefully maintained sense of normalcy. Because allowing myself to fully relive his voice threatening to kill me, or the memory of his hands around my neck, still felt capable of dismantling me entirely.

I drove past the house once more as I turned back toward the main road, forcing my breathing into something steady.

I held myself together until I merged onto the freeway.

That was when the dam broke.

Through tears I didn't realize were falling, I asked questions I knew no one could answer.

Why did the man who claimed to love me decided the day I tried to leave would be the day he tried to kill me?

Why did his eyes darken with every blow?

Why the shovel, the trash bags, the duct tape?

Why the shotgun pointed at my body?

Why the baseball bat?

Why the telephone cord around my neck?

There are no answers to questions like these. Only silence.

I pulled off the freeway and parked near a neighborhood Boys & Girls Club. For reasons I can't explain, it felt safe.

I sobbed openly, asking questions into the void while my friend listened with quiet patience, encouraging me to stay with the feelings instead of running from them.

Eventually, the storm passed.

Exhaustion replaced anger.

I quietly inhaled a breath to center myself. I wiped my face, painfully aware that life outside my car continued as normal. I took yet another breath and, for the first time, allowed myself to speak directly to him — not aloud, but inside my own mind.

You did not destroy me.

You did not steal my ability to love, to trust, or to rebuild.

You showed me darkness, yes.

You left me with shadows that still linger. I sleep with the lights on most nights. I keep rooms illuminated even when empty.

But you never extinguished my light.

As I merge back onto the freeway, I drift into a quiet conversation with myself, one that slowly turns toward what matters now — my children, my relationships, the future I am still building. It isn't perfect, and it isn't free from scars, but it is undeniably mine.

Sunlight stretches across my dashboard as warm wind moves through my open window. For the first time, I feel the memory slipping behind me instead of pulling me back toward it.

I turn up the radio, letting the music soften the noise in my head, while watching the lush green trees blur past. My exit appears ahead. A little while later, I pulled into my driveway.

I am home. This is the life he did not take from me. This is what comes after. And I am free at last

CHAPTER 56

Desperately Wanting Love

One year before I met the man who would become my husband, I wrote in my journal *"I just want to find true love. Why is it so hard to find a man who isn't afraid to love? It seems most human beings don't know how to do it in a forever kind of way..."*

I trailed off into more nonsense regarding relationships and human nature. In my seventeen-year-old mind, I had it all figured out. The secret to happiness was love. You simply had to find the right person.

Why in the world was I in such a hurry to find true love? When I wrote that, I was seventeen years old for God's sake.

This morning, over thirty years since that journal entry, I sat back in my chair and laughed out loud. Hard enough that my two dogs, lurking under my desk, looked at me in surprise. Macy tilted her head to one side while Pepper jumped up, placing her paws in my lap. I reached down and petted both of their heads.

"Girls, if only seventeen-year-old me, hadn't been such a fool!"

I turned back to the open journal on my desk, skimmed a few more lines, and closed it. I shook my head. It was starting to make sense now.

That version of me was how it became possible for him to eventually swallow me whole. My lack of experience with relationships, opened the door wide. I didn't know what was good in a relationship. What was healthy versus what wasn't. There had not been enough groundwork in my short life to lay a foundation strong enough to build anything safe.

Control and coercion were foreign to me. Those words – those behaviors – didn't exist in my mind.

It was no wonder I didn't recognize how his undying love for me was, from the very beginning, possessive.

Part of me always wanted to hang on to the idea he had fallen in love with me. That it had been authentic. That he cared about who I was and what I wanted from life. That he valued my needs alongside his own.

It always felt easier to believe the control came later. That it grew as I became more confident. More independent.

It was easier to believe his attempt to kill me came from some twisted, perverted version of love.

That is so fucked up.

Nothing makes it better. Nothing makes it easier. But believing it was a way to survive the truth.

He set out to control me from the start. That is not love.

His existence mattered more than mine. That is not love either.

I sometimes wish there had been a class back in High School that taught teenagers about relationships. Seventeen-year-old me could have gained from that. Because we don't know what we don't know until we've lived it.

I imagine classrooms filled with young girls and boys learning what love should feel like. Learning what it should never feel like. Learning what we should protect and what we should never surrender.

I am still learning, over three decades later. I am still trying to set boundaries to protect my happiness and wellbeing.

Maybe I could have learned it earlier.

Or maybe this is what life is - slowly discovering that love from another person cannot be the thing that saves us.

We have to learn to love ourselves first.

CHAPTER 57

Close Your Eyes And Let Go

When I close my eyes and go back, I see it all.

The shadows stretch across the walls. The light of day pushed in through the windows, unaware of what was unfolding beneath it. The dampness of my skin, still wet from my morning shower, gentle drips from hair barely dried – only hurriedly rubbed with a towel – sliding down the back of my neck.

Ordinary details, frozen in a moment that was anything but ordinary.

I see our bodies moving throughout the house, both of us fighting for what we wanted.

Him – my death. Me – my right to live long enough to see another sunrise. It is frantic and chaotic, yet strangely distant, as though I am watching it from somewhere just outside myself.

It becomes so quiet there when I close my eyes. The movement is rapid, desperate, rushed – but there is no sound. I don't hear myself screaming or struggling or crying. I see my mouth open. I see my body resist. But the sounds that should accompany it all are missing, as if my mind turned the volume down in order to survive.

I do hear his voice, cutting through with the threats I've already shared. And yet, over time, even those words have lost their power. They no longer echo the way they once did.

Somewhere between then and now, I poured myself another drink. The night is crisp. I am in my late forties – single, a mother of two – sitting alone at home.

It starts innocently enough.

The drinking.

Cooking dinner – there's a drink on the counter.

Eating dinner – another.

After the kitchen is clean – well, you get the idea.

I don't know exactly when alcohol became a problem. No one plans to look in the mirror one day and say out loud, "*I am an alcoholic*".

I'm not fond of labels, but honesty matters here. I may have been a highly functioning one – but nonetheless, I was one.

As I move through these memories, I've had several more drinks. A double vodka with diet coke. My drink of choice. It began years earlier with wine – just to quiet the noise, just to sleep.

Then it became anything and everything.

Tequila with friends.

Shots lined up at the bar.

Vodka while hosting.

Fireball for good measure.

I lean back into the cushions on my back porch, drink firm in my hand, my head swimming now.

When I close my eyes again, I still see the shadows of that June morning nearly thirty years ago. But they no longer frighten me. They no longer own me. I have taken my life back.

Not without suffering and consequences, however. I am jaded in ways I never planned to be. And still, I choose to believe more in the light of people than in the imagined power of those shadows.

It took a long time to wade through the pain, the obsession, the countless liquor bottles filling the recycling bin.

The pain was numbed – but the real work began when I put the bottle down. I poured the last of a half-gallon of vodka into my kitchen sink, my grown children standing as witnesses.

The sound of it rushing away felt final.

Necessary. I turned the page.

I didn't need the booze anymore. I am still fun and funny, witty and clever without it.

What I needed most was clarity – the kind that let me finally face the thousands of words written across journals, folders, books, laptops, and hard drives over the past three decades.

Only then could there be peace.

Only then could I truly walk out the front door.

There was a time I would be on my back porch, sitting back, having had one drink after the other. Now, the only drink I have is some flavored water. With a splash of an energy drink for the fizz.

I am surrounded by soft light and color, by things I built and chose and kept. The shadows don't disappear; they simply stay where they belong.

And I sit in the glow, breathing in the quiet, alive enough to notice it.

CHAPTER 58

What Is It To Be Human?

What is it to be human?

Is it compassion for others as well as ourselves?

I do not claim to have answers, but I feel compelled to try.

I still look for the good in people. I go there first. I take time to really look into a person's eyes. It's observing when they don't know someone is watching. It is the best time to truly see a person. Across a crowded room, perhaps they're smiling at the person they are engaged in a conversation with or perhaps they are sitting by themselves, lost in thought.

Look closely.

Instinct often whispers truths long before words do.

I should be jaded. I should be haunted by visions of dark sullen eyes that turned black almost, as his rage continued.

As I sit here today, I feel pity.

Not for him but for what he threw away that day. I wonder if he feels remorse. If he, in moments of solitude, understands his decision to harm me. To harm himself. To harm his family.

This was not just about us. It was not fate. It was a decision whose consequences still echo nearly thirty years later.

There is a nagging question in the back of my mind. Could I have a conversation with him today? Could I forgive him face to face?

Privately, I have had to forgive him. In journal entries . Letters he will never receive. Nobody should carry that much hate and sorrow in their heart. It only causes more harm.

The big question is if I could honestly forgive him? If he were on his death bed, could I give him that?

Would he even want it? That would have, required him to have loved me at one point and that is questionable at best. He was in love with the idea of me.

What is it to be human then? Having grace for another human is an extraordinary gift to give.

I will always carry scars, but now, what he did; it's simply something that happened to me.

I am not wrapped up in the darkness of it all today. I am knee deep in the trenches trying to write the story as best I can. But, I am not trapped anymore.

It feels clinical as my fingers fly across the keyboard.

It's more about creating something that will pull people in so they can learn from my mistakes. Using the right words and correct imagery feels important.

Perhaps it means that I am healed.

Many have questioned me about writing this book.

Is it causing more harm than good, hashing it all up again, they wonder.

I have come to understand what I am capable of and what scares me. That part of my life no longer holds any power over me. This is simply fulfilling a promise I made to myself many years ago.

Share your story.

How about a different perspective?

What if he had been given twenty-five years to life? What if he claimed he was innocent? Does that change anything? Is this where humanity enters the room?

In a parallel universe, I would show up at a parole hearing and be asked to forgive him. Accept he was an old man who possibly deserved to live the remainder of his life, outside the walls of a prison.

I do not know.

If being human requires showing compassion for others, I suspect, yes, I would do those things.

However, would I be doing it for the right reasons?

Am I trying to secure my own entry into heaven?

Jesus helped the sinner that lives in all of us, so thus the bible tells us to forgive.

The facts are this.

He is not innocent. What he has done with his life after leaving prison doesn't matter to me. If that makes me less of a human, so be it.

Only two people were in that house all those years ago. Two people who know the truth. He showed me no humanity. Why am I even considering showing him any now?

He may have lived an extraordinary life after all this. Perhaps nobody in his life today sees the diabolical man that exists just right under the surface of his skin.

I saw that man. And, it didn't appear to be human.

I am not trying to be vengeful. I am being honest.

He does not deserve my forgiveness nor my humanity. And that does not make me less human.

CHAPTER 59

I Wasn't Drowning

When I eventually became a wife again and then a mother, I wasn't drowning myself in alcohol. I was a social drinker at best. An occasional glass of wine with dinner. A margarita at a Mexican restaurant seemed appropriate. I didn't need to drown out my life.

I recall having a six pack of Zima's, an alcoholic lightly carbonated, citrus flavored beverage, in my fridge for a month. One month it took me to drink six bottles. That is not someone drowning in alcohol.

I was busy changing diapers, breastfeeding and doing laundry. Oh, the laundry. I never was good at keeping up with it back then. Today, I may have a slightly messy overstuffed walk-in closet, but I don't let laundry pile up.

Days consisted of chasing a toddler up and down the stairs. Making sure my youngest got her nap in. Cuddling up under a blanket on the sofa and reading bedtime stories. Teaching both of them the alphabet as they got older. Running them to preschool. What did I need to drown out? Nothing.

To wrap up the day, I was dancing in the living room with a baby on my hip while my toddler was learning how to move his little legs to the beat. Soaking in bathtubs, blowing bubbles and making toy cars leap off the edge into the water.

I took motherhood seriously.

I can't say I was great at it in the beginning but I grew more confident as the years passed by.

My babies became teenagers and by then, I hadn't been a wife in a very long time. Just a mom. Yes, another divorce. I was juggling work, kids, youth sports, life. Maybe not well but I managed.

Slowly, I began to drink more. Hosted birthday parties at my house. Eventually football parties. Food and drink were plenty. It was then, I began to drown just a little.

Kids needed me less and less. Bedroom doors stayed closed longer. As they became adults still living at home, dinner at the kitchen table became less frequent.

They had jobs and lives of their own. The house grew quieter in a way I had once prayed for and now didn't know what to do with. A couple of failed relationships later, many, oh so many, one-night stands, and loneliness slipped in quietly, like it had always been waiting for an invitation.

If I'm honest, that's when my friend, my companion became a regular visitor. My vodka bottle. It never argued. Never left.

Unless of course, it became an empty bottle and I would have to rush out to get another. My reliable companion was there waiting for me in the cabinet above the stove. It never asked questions I was in no mood to answer.

I didn't realize how much of myself had been poured into everyone else until I started pouring something into a glass just for me.

I began to gain weight. The woman looking back at me in my full length mirror didn't look like me.

She looked tired.

Without purpose.

She looked like she forgot to love herself.

Make-up on yes, but a body that looked foreign.

Having to buy larger size clothes was a blow to my ego. The worst part was seeing myself in photographs unless the angle was taken just right.

I would then join a gym, lose 25 lbs and things were good for a while. Eventually though, the weight came back.

A few times. The booze came back too.

The amount I would consume increased slowly. I became scared when I realized a half gallon had been drunk in the matter of four evenings.

Just me.

No guests there to help finish it.

So, I quit for thirty days. I told myself it was only for a little while. I wanted to prove to myself that I could quit drinking although deep down, I wasn't committed to it long term.

When the thirty days were up, I decided on wine. For some reason, wine would make me more tired, hence I wasn't consuming as much. That only lasted a short time.

My old friend, vodka, was missing. So, I struck up that old friendship once more. Vodka and diet-coke gave me energy surprisingly. The sharp taste of the soda mixed with the burn of the alcohol fit much better than a bottle of white zinfandel.

Hence one drink would turn into many late nights and many cocktails.

I continued to drown myself.

I was highly functioning during the day for work.

But, once I poured that drink after parking my car in the driveway, it would feel less lonely. Alcohol kept me company.

I can sit here now, in hindsight and see all of this. I ignored it blissfully while it was happening.

Today, I am almost three years free from alcohol. By the time this goes to print, I will still be sober.

Because I finally remembered how to swim.

CHAPTER 60

Motherhood; The Good, The Bad, The Ugly

Looking back over the years since becoming a mom, I find myself falling in love with my children over and over again.

With each year that rolls past – each milestone marked and survived – I breathe a little easier. Not because the job is done. God no. But because I've walked them a little farther down the road. Because they've made it another year. Because I've made it another year.

Sometimes I imagine handing over the keys to their adult lives and saying, *"Here you go. I got you this far. The rest is up to you."*

Wouldn't that be something?

Any parent reading that is probably laughing. You don't ever hand over the keys. You just move from the driver's seat to the passenger side. And even then, your foot still hovers over an imaginary brake.

Yes, I breathe easier now – but the worry never leaves.

It just changes shape.

When they were small, it was choking hazards and fevers at 2 a.m.

Now it's heartbreak.

Decisions.

The people they love. The people that love them.

The way the world can bruise them. The way a cruel world could try to break them, like the world tried to do to me all those years ago. Although, I use the word, "world" loosely here as we all know, it wasn't the world. It was a diabolical man. I never want something like this for them.

Motherhood plants a permanent knot in your gut. You're constantly asking: Am I doing this right?

Should I have done that differently? Did I protect them enough?

Did I protect them too much?

The trick to parenting isn't always stopping the fall, but assisting them up when they do. Inevitably they will fall.

I just pray I have given them the tools to get back on their feet.

We want to get it right. Every single part of it. We want to know we did everything in our power to mold and teach and love and protect the little creatures who came from our bodies.

We want to give them direction – but not too much. Cushion their falls – but not so much they never learn how to navigate their own lives.

I didn't make it to fifty-something without landing flat on my face a few times. Why would they?

We hope for fewer slammed doors. Less teenage angst. Fewer moments where they look at you like you're the enemy. We want the best for our children.

My *"offspring,"* as I sometimes call them on social media.

It makes me laugh.

It sounds scientific.

Detached.

But it's dripping with love.

They are my offspring. The ones I carried.

The ones I fought to stay alive for.

And here's the truth: I know I didn't get half of it right.

I could have done better with breakfast on school mornings. I could have packed more organic lunches. Planned more road trips. Taken them to the park more. Paid more attention on days when I was just plain exhausted.

Before anyone calls CPS – my kids were fed. They are alive. They are thriving. Besides, they are now in their twenties and a call would be too late anyhow.

What I am talking about here however, is the quiet guilt mothers carry.

The mental ledger of *"could haves."*

But here's the other truth: I always put them first.

Even when I was broken.

Even when I was scared.

Even when I was clawing my way toward sobriety.

Even when I didn't fully know who I was.

Long before they were born, two faceless children existed in my mind like a promise from the future.

"Don't give up," they seemed to say.

"We want you to be our mom."

That belief – crazy or divine – kept me here.

Now when I close my eyes, I scroll backward through time like there's a metal crank attached to my memory.

The beach. Sand stuck to wet legs.

A first-grade holiday concert – my kids on stage, scanning the crowd for my face. A soccer field – my daughter charging forward, fierce and unstoppable, teammates swarming her after the winning goal.

A baseball game with cottonwood floating so thick it looked like snow – my son diving, rolling, standing up with the ball in his glove for the final out.

The crowd cheering.

My heart exploding.

Motherhood is a treasure chest of moments. I don't remember every detail of the last twenty-plus years, but I remember the feeling.

Most of the time it feels like fuzzy winter socks when it's twenty-eight degrees outside – warm, safe, soft.

Other times it feels like you can't find the socks at all. Everything is cold and frustrating and you're questioning your entire existence.

And sometimes you find only one sock because the dryer ate the other – and that's the season of confusion. Fear. Anger. Not knowing whether you're failing them or they're just becoming who they're meant to be.

Kids are not tiny angels sent to test your patience politely. They can be cranky, selfish, dramatic, and dismissive.

They can hurt your feelings.

They can make you cry.

They can make you question why the hospital allowed you to walk out with a newborn when you had zero credentials.

Parenthood isn't pancakes on a Tuesday or perfectly behaved children who go to bed when you ask. Sometimes it's that. But more often it's messy and loud and layered with arguments you can't win against a six-year-old – or a sixteen-year-old.

It's evolving. It's learning how to fit together as human beings. It's realizing your child is not an extension of you – but a completely separate soul walking beside you for a while.

It is also respecting them as a human being, even though they are your child. It's about not always asserting your authority because you're mom or dad, but understanding they have their own emotions and opinions no matter if they are six or twenty-six.

When I was a little girl, I didn't have what most would call a traditional family. My mother was gone. My older sister stepped in. My father was there until he wasn't. Two older brothers as well. Grief woven into everything.

Maybe that's why motherhood feels like weaving threads to me.

Every year, I take the threads that define my son and the threads that define my daughter and I try to weave them gently into the fabric of who I am as their mother. Adjusting.

Repairing. Reinforcing. Learning as I go.

This is the first time I am a mother to a child of this particular age.

For each year that passes, we grow in ways not always easy to have language for. But, we figure it out as we go along.

Together.

The tapestry is not perfect. But it's strong.

I'm grateful that my children know me – the real me. Sometimes better than I know myself. They've seen my flaws.

My fights.

My failures.

They’ve seen me fall and stand back up.

And maybe that’s part of getting it right. Not perfection.

Presence.

We will still fall. All of us. But I like to think that after all these years, there are just enough cushions scattered across the floor to soften the landing.

And if not?

We’ll get back up anyway. United.

CHAPTER 61

The Things That Wait Patiently

While I built a life, my trauma and memory quietly waited. Some nights, it would show up in my dreams. Other times, it would appear in the way that I responded to conflict with other people.

I have learned that trauma is incredibly patient. It does not clap its hands together loudly, demanding attention. It waits in the silent spaces, sometimes for decades, until life becomes still enough that it finally can be heard.

I never understood that my quick to anger responses were never about the fact a friend hadn't called in a long time. It didn't have anything to do with the fact that my teenager hadn't picked up his room or brought dirty dishes down after multiple days.

Those were things that could be explained or handled easily. A quick call to my friend telling her I missed her; and she would explain the demands of her family and work has just kept her busy. The lack of a phone call was not intentional.

My teenager will simply bring down his dirty dishes, load the washer and that's the end of the problem. There is no need for shouting. There is no reason for disappointment or anger.

My reactions were often echoes of the past.
Fragmented sounds of a conflict from a different version of my life. It was not what was happening in front of me, but of moments where my voice had been swallowed entirely.

I was responding as every version of myself that had ever felt unheard, unsafe, or trapped with nowhere safe to put the fear. I avoided fear because in my survivor mindset, I was not allowed to be fearful of anything.

Of course, I knew nothing of this for years.

It was simply there, right under the surface of my skin, waiting to jump out and explain itself.

Because I had fought the beast and won, nobody could touch me. Not the physical me or the emotional me.

Both of them were placed under strict protection.

High security at all times.

Often as if in solitary confinement.

I was someone who tried to sail through life. Not in the traditional sense. I worked hard for everything we had and provided for my family.

What I mean is, I tried to ignore my deepest pain. The pain knowing that he truly had wanted me dead.

That nearly broke me.

I have read the legal documents from all of those weeks and months, when they were building a case against him.

There is a common denominator that keeps showing up.

His intent.

It's right there, on the papers in front of me now, almost thirty years later. What is not anywhere to be found, is his why? Nowhere does he apologize or explain he wasn't really trying to murder me. Which leads me to know without a doubt, he actually wanted me dead.

I despise death. I fear it most of all. When there is nothing.

When I cease to exist.

That is why I drank.

To try to forget how close I was. There is nowhere in my mind where I can reconcile how or why he came to that decision. I cannot fathom it. That's the demon that chases me down unfamiliar hallways and into darkened rooms where he waits silently. Until he takes one step forward, from behind the shadows, and grins at me. His eyes are completely black. His smile immediately fades and then I see the shotgun.

Nobody wants this. Everyone would avoid those images any way possible. I chose to do so with my good old friend and companion, my vodka bottle. Prior to that, she was a bottle of white zinfandel.

Some days, I could spew it all out, spilling my hurt, my fears, my wanting to just sink deep into my bed and stay there for hours.

Take another sip.

"That's better", I would think.

"He's no longer there. His intent has been removed and I am not dying..." I whisper out loud to no one.

It would always catch up with me later. Maybe not the next day or the following week, but six months later it might come up again.

The booze would eventually catch up though. In the form of exhaustion or a cold. Never a hangover per se. Over time, I became a professional. Not in what I needed to be though.

I was a woman with many skills, yet a master of none. If anything, I had become an expert in sweeping everything under the rug.

How ironic.

Isn't that what I accused his defense attorney of doing all those years ago?

Here it is finally.

I want everyone reading this to pause. Just for a moment before continuing. I want you to really hear this. Can you do that for me?

As a survivor, this part is difficult to ascertain, yet this is so important.

Avoidance will feel like survival for a very long time. AVOIDANCE. Let me repeat it so you see it clearly.

I told myself that moving forward meant not looking back. What I did not understand was that memories left untouched do not fade. They preserve themselves. Perfectly intact.

Like a jar of homemade peaches. The color might be a little off from the original, fresh fruit. But, it's there waiting for you to twist the lid until it makes that all familiar popping sound.

They are ready for you now.

Just like all those memories you shoved deep down. They never left you.

They were there. Waiting for the moment when you finally stop running long enough to notice they are still standing right behind you. Or beside you.

Embrace them all.

I have now, almost three decades later.

Sit in all the shit and be present with yourself for once.

Without any kind of substance to push you one way or another. Sit in the middle of it. Only then can you dismantle everything before beginning to put pieces back together.

I am now aware that sobriety did not create my memories. It simply removed the fog that allowed me to pretend they weren't there. As I continue putting the broken pieces of myself back together, I am only choosing the ones that still belong to me.

It doesn't have to be a masterpiece I am building.

It just has to be honest. The authentic version of me is far more trustworthy than the woman standing on a stage, loudly singing a karaoke song she barely knows.

Some days, the memories still sit quietly beside me. They don't shout anymore. They don't chase me through dark hallways. They simply wait to be acknowledged before settling back into their place.

I have learned something I wish I had understood much earlier. Trauma doesn't wait to hurt you.

It waits until you are safe enough to feel it.

CHAPTER 62

Housekeeping

The vacuum moving gently over the carpet in front of me is barely audible.

In my ears, sit two simple pink and white earbuds, and the sound of a woman's voice drowns out the vacuum motor's hum.

I push and move across the space, then stop to unlatch the extension wand to suck up a piece of forgotten cracker tucked away in the corner. Once back into the vacuum base, I keep moving the appliance across the floors. My body knows this work even when my mind wanders elsewhere as the woman in my ears keeps talking.

From carpet to hardwoods, from hardwoods to linoleum in bathrooms. Sometimes from gray granite tile to bright white shiny ones.

As if we are one, my vacuum and I travel behind sofas, in between a washer and dryer, underneath the kitchen table and in corners forgotten since I was last there, two weeks ago.

Soon I am wiping the insides of a toilet, especially up underneath where the water enters from inside the bowl with a rag or a brush. I eventually move to bathtubs and showers, sinks and grout.

I bend, I lean, I wipe, I scrub.

And, then as I exit the space, I flip the lights off behind me. My hand expertly reaches back knowing right where the light switches are as if this is my own house. Upon my departure from each space, there is a calculated scent of clean left behind. Sometimes a floral cleaner chosen by the homeowner, other times a strong smell of bleach or ammonia. Never both of the latter two in the same place though. That can be a deadly concoction.

The woman in my ears drones on about this and that, expanding on the story that began about forty-five minutes ago. I continue listening with my mind half there in the audible story and the rest of me focusing on the job in front of me. The day goes by quickly as I push my body up and down stairs, in corners, sometimes on top of a small step ladder to remove an annoying cobweb and even crawling on all fours and hand mopping an unusually sticky floor.

It's all part of my occupation. An occupation that I fell into a couple years after leaving photography behind.

"Hi, how's your day so far? Housekeeping, reporting for duty".

I giggle at this thought flashing in my brain as I have never actually said that to a client in the many years I've been coming to their homes week after week and year after year.

When I first started, it was out of survival and the need to provide for my family. It was half-hearted at best, but always with the intent of doing good work. I never imagined I would be doing it for over a decade. I wasn't a little girl growing up in Norway, dreaming that one day I would grow up to clean other peoples spaces.

Life can be messy, some places more than others, and someone should clean it. Why not me and get paid for it all the same?

As a little girl back on the other side of the world, I remember getting my first camera from my father on my birthday. What year it was escapes me. Later I would grow to use a bigger camera given to me by my brother-in-law so I guess you could say, photography was the dream at one point.

My other dream was writing.

Yet, back then I did not have the language for it.

I really didn't know what to write about. And, I never could have imagined I would be writing about the day my husband would attempt to kill me. That most definitely, was never the dream.

Over the years, I learned tricks of the trade and eventually mastered my schedule and created a very successful operation. It is a part of my life, yet it doesn't define who I am as a person.

In many ways while my hand scrubs a surface, my mind writes. I am constantly working on a plethora of thoughts while moving throughout a client's space.

It is important to note that my clients never make me feel less than. As a matter of fact, I am treated with the utmost respect. Conversations with them all over the years, come from a place of caring about one another.

It's a mutual level of care and it's an intimate relationship if you truly look at it. I am invited into people's homes, in their private spaces that houseguests will never enter.

That respect isn't lost on me and as they trust me, I trust them right back. They keep me *"employed"* and with that, there is gratitude.

About six years ago or perhaps it was more, I started sharing with my clients that I was writing a book.

Again.

And, this time I will complete it.

In fact, I hoped that it would have been done by the time I turned fifty. Well, the best of plans don't always land at the intended destination.

As time passes us by, we find ourselves in situations that may not be exactly where we wish to be. Even though it continues to serve us and others, it isn't the dream.

Perfect vacuum lines are not my dream. Nor is the smell of bleach encompassing my nostrils. I love the flexibility of my owner-operated business, yet in the back of my mind, there has always been a nagging thought that I could be so much more.

More than just *"housekeeping."* That is not to say there is anything wrong with this occupation. It is simply to say, I want more.

More than clean toilets and shiny stainless steel appliances.

The podcast has come to an end and I hear the exit credits in my ears. My vacuum has been put away and the mop in my hand is currently being placed back in the utility room.

I put on my jacket or hoodie depending on the season, pick up my backpack with my water, lunch box, a few protein bars and a banana I neglected to eat.

The clients are not home on this day, so after I bring my vacuum and supplies outside the front door, I lock up after a final inspection inside and a mental checklist that my tasks are complete for the day.

Soon, I am in my SUV making my way home or some days a quick trip to Costco for some laundry soap. My hamper is full and clothes need washing.

As the wheels finally stop in my driveway about an hour and fifteen minutes after leaving my clients home, I take a deep breath.

My body feels tired, yet accomplished.

There were perfect vacuum lines today and that makes me smile at my reflection in the hall mirror just inside my own front door.

This wasn't the life I dreamed, but nonetheless it is my life. I am proud of all that I have accomplished in the past three decades; whether that being a photographer or simply "housekeeping" doesn't matter.

I am inhabiting a life I didn't plan and I refuse to let it erase me regardless of my title.

The fact I am here at all is the victory I celebrate every day.

CHAPTER 63

The Perfectly Imperfect Me

I used to drink a lot. I also used to hurt people. Not physically, but emotionally. I never set out to hurt anyone, yet I know now, I left wounds in people who never asked for them.

It's the funny thing about abusing alcohol. We think we become more fun, more entertaining and the life of the party, when in reality it is the farthest from the truth.

Under flashing lights, while throwing our bodies across the dance floor, the fun is an illusion yet it keeps us coming back over and over again. We are actors in our own lives, performing something that isn't real. The rush of the moment is all that matters. Not people's feelings from your crass words or the joke that didn't land as you intended.

When I used to drink at the bar, the bartenders knew what I wanted to drink and kept them coming. More nights than I would like to admit, I would close the place down, then leave with a faceless stranger for his house at 2 am.

Many sunrises went unappreciated as I would seek out my clothes strewn all over an unfamiliar floor, dressing quickly before that particular *"date"* woke and I would hurry to my car to make my way home to get ready for work or a lazy day sleeping it off.

Like I said, I hurt people.

I am not proud of this version of me.

Yet, I have to own that woman.

I used to convince myself that alcohol made me brave. That it made me fearless and untouchable in ways I never felt when I was sober. It softened the sharp edges of memories I did not want to revisit. It quieted the voice inside me that asked questions I did not want to answer. And, if only for a few hours, I could become someone lighter.

I know now, I was the loudest person in the room. I never meant it to take someone else's voice away. I wanted so desperately to be seen and heard. My mistake was thinking that alcohol made me more likeable when in fact, the opposite was true.

The truth is, alcohol didn't remove any of my demons. It simply dimmed the lights so I could pretend they were not standing beside me.

When I drank, I became a more reckless version of myself. I chased connection in all the wrong places because it felt easier than sitting alone with my thoughts. I mistook attention for affection and chaos for excitement. In those moments, I wasn't searching for strangers.

I was searching for escape.

The escape only lasted so long before I had to return to my regular, boring self and the disco lights wouldn't turn on.

There were mornings, after leaving yet another faceless *"date"*, that I would sit in my car outside my house, gripping the steering wheel before going inside. I would try to piece together the night before like fragments of a broken mirror, hoping nothing I said or did had shattered someone else in the process.

Sometimes I remembered. Sometimes I didn't.

In many ways, not knowing was worse. It would cause me to panic and I could think of nothing else for days.

Until of course, I was right back out there, looking for *"Mr. Right"*.

"Mr. Right", right now, was more like it.

Because, I knew, although I thought I wanted more, I never even gave them a chance to prove they weren't *"Mr. Wrong"*.

Alcohol gave me permission to outrun pain, but it also allowed me to outrun accountability. And while I never raised a hand to another person, I know now that words, absence, and emotional carelessness can leave bruises just as deep.

Owning that truth is uncomfortable.

It forces me to stand face to face with a version of myself I would rather pretend never existed.

But healing is not about rewriting who we were.

It is about acknowledging her, understanding her, and choosing to grow beyond her.

Even now, sitting here having not touched a drink in what will be three years this October, I still fear I have so much to find peace with. I am aware that I have to forgive that old version of me, because not doing so serves no one. Just because I have had more sexual partners in my lifetime than most, it doesn't make me a bad person.

It simply means I am a good person who did some not-so-good things with strangers I will most likely never see again.

Frankly, most probably forgot my name as soon as I offered it at the bar, while slinging back shots of tequila during last call. Yet, again, I have to own that version of me in order to move forward.

I am not sure when the cracks started showing themselves.

I think it might have been a particularly boring date with some guy I met off a dating site. The conversation was dull, so I kept ordering more drinks. He didn't seem to notice at first and I certainly didn't give it much thought as the evening progressed. I was trying to make something out of nothing. When we made it out to the parking lot, he kissed me on the cheek, told me to get home safely.

I never heard from him again.

Here's the interesting part though. The date was boring and I had spent the entire night drinking, trying to make it more fun. I probably became that version of myself, that now looking back, terrifies me. Not in a scary way. The embarrassing kind. If that isn't a red flag for any man, I don't know what is.

As I downed my fifth vodka-diet, he probably decided he should end it right there. I don't blame him. I don't even blame myself.

I couldn't see it until I was finally forced to look at it.

Instead of punishing myself now for a past that I can't erase, I am simply going to write about it. In doing so, I hope that if any of those faceless strangers were to read this, they can see my intent to sleep with them for a night and basically throw them away the following day, was not done so with malice.

In trying to piece together blurry nights that turned into sunlit mornings without success, there was an emotional punishment I most certainly bestowed onto myself. If obsessing over what I may or may not have done isn't punishment, then I don't know what is. It's the not knowing that becomes your worst nightmare.

There was a time I lacked power over my body.

When I was told I was too fat. That I wasn't sexy enough. When I in fact was very thin and probably a little bit sexy.

When I was told, I simply wasn't good enough. In every way.

I was told that he would be the only one that could ever love me. He would be the one who could keep me safe from my grief. He was the only lover I would ever need. The only one who claimed he could touch me in ways that brought pleasure — yet today, I have no memory of that.

Perhaps because in the end, his touch was violent and brutal. It erased any memory of a time that didn't align with that version of him.

Before he tried to kill me, there was also a time when he took my body without permission. I am sure he never viewed it in that light. I was his wife after all. His disregard for the ownership of my body, still brings me pain today. It was never his to do with as he pleased.

But, he did it anyway. That is not love. That is not marriage.

That is rape.

As distance grew between that life and this new one, many years later, I was acting out my mid-life rebellion. In seeking these sexual encounters, a part of me was trying to prove that other men would see me.

They would love me. We all know sex equals love. Of course it doesn't.

Yet, it became a substitute and one I could control. I could control what I drank and who I slept with. These were my choices and not anyone else's. The sex was fun and exhilarating in ways that made me feel alive.

It gave me back the power over my body. There's an undercurrent of something beautiful there, no matter how some people may view me. I am ok with that and will stand tall in that judgement.

I don't drink anymore. I also try not to hurt people. I am a different woman today. And, I forgive her, because she was surviving the only way she knew how.

CHAPTER 64

The Quiet Ways Control Takes Root

As a young woman more than thirty years ago, I had no business playing house with a thirty-three-year-old man.

I know that now.

At eighteen, I was in a hurry to grow up and far too inexperienced to recognize the quiet ways control can take root.

There is a common misconception that strong, independent women are immune to this kind of abuse.

In truth, strength can be the very thing that attracts someone intent on control. There is no challenge in dominating someone who already doubts herself. But a woman who is confident, ambitious, and capable presents something to conquer.

The process is rarely obvious. It unfolds slowly — so slowly it can be mistaken for the natural evolution of life. After all, we are taught that change is inevitable. We are less often taught to question who is steering it.

He never hit me during our marriage until, well that day. Not once.

Compared to what so many women endure, it would be easy to dismiss what happened as minor. His weapons were quieter — cutting remarks, subtle criticism, and an ever-tightening grip on my independence.

At the time, I believed it was love. I believed we were building toward the dream: a home, children, and a shared future. Looking back, I see he did not want to build a life with me. He wanted a life that revolved entirely around him.

I often find myself wondering what his endgame was, though I know I will never have that answer. We were together for nearly six years. As he approached forty, he spoke casually about children — always someday, never now. That promise became a horizon that never seemed to come closer.

Much of those six years exists in fragments in my memory, as if my mind quietly decided certain details were not worth keeping.

I remember him working in his shop, surrounded by outboard motors, rusted engines, and various pieces of machinery he insisted still had value. He bought and sold these things constantly, often using money that came from my inheritance after my parents died.

The profits, if they existed, never found their way back to me. At eighteen, grief and love blurred my judgment, and I handed over resources meant to secure my future without hesitation.

Only years later did I begin connecting the contradictions. He spoke of waiting to start a family until we were financially stable, yet we had the means to buy a home if that money had not vanished into his projects.

Stability was never truly the goal. Delay was.

Recently, I found an old journal with a list of goals written between 1993 and 1995. What struck me most was not what I wrote — but what I didn't.

My marriage was nearly absent from those pages. My instincts tell me I was afraid he might read my private thoughts, so I slowly stopped recording them.

Earlier entries speak with certainty and devotion. I declared him my forever. I signed entries with *"I love you, Honey,"* as though I was writing love letters to him. In a book meant only for myself. I don't know why I felt compelled to perform love even in solitude.

One entry stopped me cold. Dated May 17, 1995 — one year before he attempted to kill me — I wrote:

"I guess I can't read people very well anymore. Nothing else is new, this about covers it. I do have many things on my mind, but I don't really want to write them down. There are a few things left unsaid and ought to stay that way."

I then wrote the following, written in Norwegian. So he wouldn't be able to understand it if he were to ever snoop.

"I wish things were different in my life, but this is for the best, I guess. My life would be strange without my husband, yet I know that I have changed so much in the last year or so. I am not the same person I once was."

That woman writing those words knew something was wrong, even if she could not safely say it out loud.

I no longer recognized myself. The girl who met him the day after her eighteenth birthday had slowly faded. Of course, no one remains the same between eighteen and twenty-three, but this was different.

This was erosion, not growth.

Now, approaching my mid-fifties, I see the distance more clearly.

Sobriety has forced me to meet versions of myself I spent years trying to outrun. I am learning to forgive the woman who eventually turned to alcohol to numb confusion and grief.

She was not reckless or careless.

She was hurting. And didn't even truly know why she was hurting.

Sometimes sadness turned into anger. Anger towards myself. Sometimes at other people.

It made no sense. No rhyme or reason.

Strangely, I did not drink much during my marriage. Alcohol would enter my life many years later-when he was far removed from me. I didn't even touch it after our relationship began dissolving into something resembling a strained roommate arrangement.

When I first voiced wanting a separation, he began introducing alcohol — a beer with dinner, a glass of wine when we went out. I cannot say with certainty what his intentions were, but the timing has never sat comfortably with me.

Our life together was, on the surface, ordinary.

We went to dinners, occasionally socialized with other couples, attended car shows and flea markets that held little interest for me, and took long Sunday drives that felt more like obligations than adventures. Most days, it was just the two of us, living in a quiet isolation I did not recognize at the time.

I built my photography business while he worked as a mechanic. Eventually, he became my assistant at wedding shoots. At the time, I believed it was support. Looking back, I suspect it was surveillance disguised as partnership.

There were dinners at his parents' house and interactions with extended family, though those memories are faint and indistinct, like photographs left too long in sunlight.

What stands out most, in retrospect, is how young I truly was.

I was still in high school when we lived together.

I graduated while sharing a home with a grown man. I see now how absolutely ridiculous that was. A thirty-three year old man had honestly no business, moving an eighteen year old girl into his house. None.

I attended college briefly before launching my photography business. We married the summer I turned twenty, a milestone that felt like adulthood but was, in many ways, an extension of adolescence shaped by someone else's expectations.

Reading through those scattered journal entries now unsettles me greatly. I appear happy or at least determined to sound happy.

I will never know if those words reflected truth or self-protection. What I do know is that my silence grew louder each year. The less I trusted him, the less I trusted myself to record what I felt.

It is a strange experience, revisiting that time and realizing how much of daily life has vanished from memory. Part of me wishes I had documented more. A larger part understands why I didn't. Forgetting, in its own way, can be a form of survival.

If anything, I wish there was more that I could turn over in my hands and inspect. Inspect for what, I'm not sure.

Nonetheless, I should have listened to my sister's warnings.

Today, I regret I didn't, yet if one thing is altered, everything that happens after, also will not be the same. I don't want to imagine a life without my now grown children.

For that, control had to be a part of my story.

And, I have made peace with that.

CHAPTER 65

An Afternoon In The Sun

My eyes flickered open yet immediately closed again as the bright sun blinded me. I keep them closed as I adjust the ridiculously large sunglasses I'm sporting.

I'm in vacation mode. A trip to the Lonestar state at least once a year to see my best friend and her family.

I hear voices and laughter close by.

Water splashing. Some birds chirped too.

There's an ever so slight breeze tickling my skin.

It's a gorgeous day and it's too bad I'm leaving today on an airplane. There's still time though.

To be still. To not think. To not ponder the massive manuscript sitting next to me on the bench. I've been sharing part of it with my best friend.

Not everything.

Just a few chapters really.

She lives a four and a half hour plane ride away and the first night here, we stayed up till past two am.

Or was it closer to four? Nobody knows.

We shared things phone calls can't properly handle.

We got into our swim suits and went swimming at around 1 am.

Laughter. Fun. Friendship.

Yet, all without a drop of alcohol. It was a test for me really. I passed. And imagine that; we had a total blast.

Sober.

Her out of respect for my sobriety.

Me because of a pinky promise.

And she likes the few things I shared in my manuscript.

"You are such a great writer" she's said more times than I can count. More reason to get off my ass and finish it, I thought to myself as she's reflecting on whatever chapter I had just shared.

"Hey, you're getting a bit red, Wifey?" a half laughing voice brings me out of my sun slumber.

"Perfect! That was the goal, Wifey! To go home to Seattle with a tan!" I respond; the perfect smart ass response I know my best friend is expecting. Both of us using the nickname our friends gave us years back since we spent so much time at each other's houses while her husband was working out of state. Wifey. Bestie. Same thing.

She laughs at my wanting to get a tan and I hop up and jump in the pool. I never want this day to end.

Later that day, when I'm on my flight back home, I'm again reading through my paper print-out of my book. It's then I know, I really have to finish it.

Thank goodness for a bestie, a plane ride, a quick five day long weekend trip, sunshine and some determination.

Did I mention I met my best friend in High School? She was the one who explained to *not* ask our math teacher what the word *"cum"* meant. We didn't hang out back then but found each other almost twenty years ago now. Seventeen years to be exact.

We have seen our kids grow up.

Seen things fall apart.

Seen things get put back together.

That's one heck of a great reason to walk through that front door and finish what I started.

By next Spring I tell myself.

Six months from now. Maybe seven.

As the plane lands, I pack my book back into my bag. But, I know, today marks the beginning of an ending.

It's now or never.

Definitely now, I say inwardly as I smile at the flight attendants while departing through the open door of a Boeing 737.

CHAPTER 66

It Was January

Stories do not live only in memory. They live in mornings like this one.

It is January, many years later and outside there is that familiar layer of frost on the grass outside my kitchen window. It sparkles slightly as the morning sun sneaks out from behind the shadows of trees surrounding the property.

Mornings no longer arrive with dread or fog, but with clarity I once thought belonged to other people.

As my hand wraps around the red mug filled to the brim with a fresh coffee, I am reminded once again, how blessed I am to be here. I see a squirrel race across the fence and another following behind. The day is just beginning and the world is waking up outside my window. I am struck, though, with how this view is so simple, it is a quiet blessing all on its own.

A lifetime has passed in the last thirty years, and so much has unfolded since. I am not exactly where I once imagined I would be, but I have learned to measure life differently.

I count blessings now, not milestones. And there have been many blessings since that fateful day.

As I have previously shared, I became a mother to two incredible children – a son and a daughter. My daughter recently got engaged, so soon I'll have a son-in-law, I get the honor of calling my "kid" too. Watching them grow into the people they are today has given me more than I ever understood motherhood could offer.

There is a quiet awe in witnessing your children become adults—learning, maturing, and discovering who they want to be in this world. They know they are loved and they stand on solid ground.

And though life will continue to shape them, as it does all of us, they carry good hearts into the world.

I am beyond proud to be their mother.

And if I'm honest, like any parent, I sometimes smile and wonder what it must be like to have me as a mom—but their love reassures me more than words ever could.

Maybe the worry comes from knowing how deeply I wanted this role and how hard I fought for motherhood. It feels like a quiet full circle—once fighting to survive, now hoping I've nurtured well.

They know my story about my first husband. Not every detail, but enough. If anything, it has given them awareness – an understanding of what love should and should not look like. I suppose I tried to teach them that pain can be a teacher if you let it.

My second husband and their father have always been present in their lives. Though we have been divorced for many years now, he is a good man and a devoted dad. That is a truth I speak with sincerity.

Part of my healing came from the simple fact that someone was willing to take a chance on me when my past felt heavy and complicated.

After the dust settled on that fateful day so many years ago, I did learn to trust and love again because of the grace and patience he showed me. Although our marriage ended in divorce a few years later, he gave me the greatest gifts of my life: our children.

For that, I will always carry gratitude. If he ever reads these words, I hope he knows that he was part of my path back toward trust, toward normalcy, toward believing life could hold good things again.

Marriage is not currently part of my life. Perhaps it will be some day but it isn't something that I am actively looking for.

Perhaps some parts of me still carry old bruises, still learning how to trust fully. To let someone in completely.

First and foremost, I need to complete this journey for me. I need to take time in front of an imaginary mirror and truly see the woman I have become, yet forgiving the girl I once was.

There is grace to be given here, not only for the people in my life that love me, but also for myself.

I am no longer that naïve girl who leaped across the world to build a life in a different country. She is still here with me though, tucked into the folds of my skin.

Sometimes she appears when life feels frightening or uncertain. When she does, I take her gently by the shoulders, turn her toward the mirror, and remind her of who she has become.

Beautiful.

Strong.

Competent.

Capable.

Free from the demons that chased her for far too long.

CHAPTER 67

Why Addiction Finds Us

It is unusually warm for this time of year. Sixty-four degrees. By lunchtime, the sun had brightened as I maneuvered my way through the winding staircase with my vacuum.

I had paused for a moment to admire the spring-like feeling outside the large windows in the sitting room before making my way upstairs. Smiling to myself, I continued up the staircase, sucking up stubborn pine needles trapped in the carpet runner.

My thoughts drifted back a few decades, and I began to wonder when I in fact had begun drinking heavily.

In my early twenties, it was not on my radar. As a high school kid — and sadly younger – yes, I had tried alcohol, sometimes a lot of it, but it never became part of my life back then.

During my marriage, it was only toward the end that he would suggest we stop at a bar for a drink or a beer. We rarely did, as the marriage was already failing, and I sensed alcohol wouldn't change our situation. If anything, it would only delay the inevitable. There would be no reconciliation between my estranged husband and me.

After shooting a wedding together one Saturday, I found myself in the passenger seat as he was supposed to be driving us back to the house.

Instead, we ended up in the middle of nowhere. He parked the car in a field, reached behind the driver's seat, and pulled out a small cooler. It was beginning to grow dark, and I felt an unease forming somewhere deep inside me. I most definitely did not wish to be in this unfamiliar place with him.

"What are we doing here?" I said, annoyance dripping from my voice.

"Let's just head back to the house."

He looked at me, smiling, and opened the cooler, revealing a couple of sandwiches and a few bottles of beer.

"I thought we could eat and enjoy a couple of beers together first," he said.

"I don't want either," I replied.

"Besides, you are driving, and drinking is probably not a great idea if you're going to continue driving."

He drove us back, and I couldn't wait to get out of that car. It may, in fact, have been the last time he worked a wedding with me before so much happened.

I am at the top of the staircase now and need to change outlets. I've lost some weight lately, and quickly, much lighter than before, hopped down the steps to unplug the cord from the wall in the downstairs hallway.

Once the vacuum hums again, although slightly muted due to my ear buds playing a new audio book in my ears, I am again pondering when my drinking began.

It wasn't after he was sentenced, and not even after he was released from prison after only serving about five years of his 7.7666 year sentence. I was probably a social drinker at best during this time and it was probably more like in my mid to late thirties, early forties, it became more.

Whether it was out at the bar with friends singing karaoke or on a date with a prospect off a dating site, the drinks would definitely flow.

There was a time I dated a man who spent most afternoons at the bar for happy hour and when I could, I would join him. I could have married that man, but it wasn't meant to be. He will always be the one that got away.

More time passed. Once upon a time, I would pick up a large bottle of wine to bring home after work. Eventually, those bottles turned into half-gallons of vodka paired with a case of Diet Coke for a mixer. If we gathered with friends on weekends, I would bring my drink of choice, often planning to stay the night so at least I would not drink and drive.

A few times, I attempted sober months and even succeeded. But once those thirty days ended, I would quietly return to drinking.

It felt less like a choice and more like a habit built from loneliness and boredom. I felt my life drifting past me. I knew I was capable of more and tried to dull the ache of not living up to my own potential.

I would pour a drink after getting home from work and unwind on the back porch by myself. Once dinner was simmering on the stove, I would make another.

When we sat down to eat, my glass was filled once again. You get the idea. By the time the kitchen was cleaned up and my family tucked into bed, a few more would grace my cup.

I would crawl into bed and fall into a slumber of drunkenness, exhaustion and knowing full well, the morning would come too soon. I would get up, do all the things required of me after a couple cups of coffee and then after arriving home after work, the cycle would repeat itself.

I've moved on from the vacuum to wiping down the bathroom mirror. I catch my reflection and instinctively, smile and stick my tongue out. All this going down memory lane tells me I am very happy I am now celebrating over two years of sobriety.

As a woman in her fifties and a single mother of two grown children, I am finally finding my footing. I have found the voice I always knew existed and learned how to show up for myself in ways I never had before.

Alcohol became a mixture of numbing pain, manufacturing fun, and filling an emptiness I did not know how to face. I was always busy. Always productive. Always highly functioning.

I was never the woman adding vodka to morning coffee. I was more of a Bloody Mary on Sunday morning kind of girl, followed by another as bacon, eggs, Norwegian pancakes, and country potatoes filled the breakfast table.

Eventually, alcohol became my substitute for a partner. When I finally heard how absurd that sounded out loud, I knew something had to change.

I close the front door after a quick goodbye to the woman inside.

"See you next month", I said cheerfully before making my way to my car. I load all my things inside and once behind the wheel, I turn on a country music station.

It's then that I realize, it doesn't matter when I began drinking too much or why it became such a big part of my daily life. I know now that I was trapped in a continuous cycle that eventually would destroy everything I have built.

It could eventually tear my relationship with my grown children to shreds and keep me slightly distant from my siblings back home. I don't want that. I want to grow all the relationships in my life, not tear them apart due to being drunk half the time.

I never wanted that life. Although it was mostly hidden from the casual observer, those that knew me, saw what I couldn't see.

I am not trapped today, hiding behind a bottle.

Today when I lay down at night, my head cocooned into my pillow and surrounded by my pets, I no longer spin tall drunken stories in my mind while falling asleep, teetering over a cliff that threatens to swallow me whole.

CHAPTER 68

Creating New Spaces

It has taken me almost thirty years to clear the trash out of my life.

I have been carting around pictures, old documents and God knows what else, stored in random boxes, living in the garage of my home and unbeknownst to me, it has kept me trapped in so many ways.

Now that it is all gone, I feel the sense of freedom it brings from not having it around anymore, although it was always out of sight so hence out of mind. Then again, it was still there and probably gave me anxiety I was unaware of.

I've sorted through pieces of this life before. There have been quiet trips to the dump over the years, small purges of the past.

But this entire project feels different. As I now sit in this new space, I am stripped of the weight I didn't realize I was still carrying. Every box and every forgotten paper has been carted away. Gone at last.

The wedding dress is gone too.

The dress that once made me feel beautiful while quietly holding the memory of everything I needed to escape. I kept it sealed in a box like it was something sacred.

In truth, it was a relic of a life that nearly broke me. I will never understand why it remained stored away all these years.

Now it sits in a landfill, buried among discarded things, exactly where it belongs. I am the only woman who will ever wear it and that feels right.

I thought about selling it over the years but I couldn't shake the feeling that it carried too much sorrow stitched into its seams. There was no way I could hand that story to another woman, even unknowingly.

I imagine her wearing it, glowing the way I did – beautiful, happy, certain of the future.

And then the picture cracks wide open, because I know how that story ends. The man waiting for me at the altar would try to take my life only a few years later.

If I'm honest, the woman I am now looks back at the woman who kept that dress and gently scolds her.

Not with cruelty – but with the kind of knowing that only comes from surviving what she hadn't yet learned how to name.

Still, I want to shake a finger at her while shaking my head.

I know that I am not the only person on this planet that has a garage filled with random crap.

More than likely, most garages are like what mine used to look like. Every garage in America probably.

Is it because we don't know how to part with things or that we become lazy; so that rather than go through things, we let them pile up to the point where it becomes such a daunting task to tackle, we turn a blind eye, walk away and leave it to be dealt with another day?

I find it difficult to put into words how this purge has made me feel. It's as if another door has been opened. However mythical that door is, it feels slightly real at the same time.

I sit here knowing I not only removed crap from my life, I am taking charge of it. My life that is. It's true that spaces can keep us trapped and once a space no longer serves you, it's time to clear that space.

Create a space that will and can serve you. And, serve you better.

Think of it this way. You build a life with someone, and when it ends, pieces of them still linger in your home like old demons or better yet, ghosts, you don't notice at first.

A chair.

A sweatshirt.

A box of books.

Time passes and they become just things. Harmless and invisible things stored out of sight.

Until one day you pick something up and it hits you—you would never have chosen this, never bought it, never loved it.

And then you remember who did.

With that realization comes the sting and the tightness in your chest. The flicker of old hurt you thought you buried. It's not a dramatic or loud experience; it's just enough to knock the wind out of you for a moment.

So you throw it away. Not because it's a book, but because it's a tether. A small thread still ties you to a version of yourself that you walked away from years ago. When it lands in the trash, it feels like taking a breath you didn't realize you'd been holding.

That is how I feel tonight. I won't be blindsided by some forgotten object that leaves me crumpled on my bedroom floor or parked by the lake trying to outrun memories that creep in anyway. I've been to those places. I know what it costs to stay there too long.

The demons may still know my name and they may still knock from time to time, but I've stopped leaving the door unlocked.

I've cleared out the boxes they used to hide in.

CHAPTER 69

Messy And Beautiful

We are all fighting the same fight – trying to find our own path and our own reasons for it all. I'm not the first person to have had something awful happen to them and I will not be the last. I've said that for more than two decades, and it's funny how now everyone is saying it.

We all have a story to tell.

Life is just a series of events that happen to and around us. Today, I do what I need to do to be happy.

I work.

I make dinners.

Sometimes.

With kids grown, there's less dinners now.

I run a household – with adult kids, dogs and cats. Some days I don't sit down until after 9 p.m. I listen to music and podcasts. I listen to audio books. I work on social media after work. A part of my routine. It's a busy life. I like being busy. Projects ARE my middle name. If there isn't one, trust me, I will find one.

Sometimes I watch mindless television in bed late at night. Sometimes I drive around the block a few extra minutes just to be with myself before returning home after work.

Occasionally, when I have the house to myself, I walk around naked.

Sometimes I turn the music up high and dance like a crazy person in my kitchen while my two dogs look at me as if I've lost my mind.

Sometimes I sit outside on my back patio for hours, smoking one cigarette after another. Because I can. Although it is a habit I do want to rid myself of. Eventually.

Other days I work in the yard, watering flowers and tending to plants. I have no idea how to grow them other than giving them water and hoping for the best.

When I wake up in the morning, I sniff out the coffee maker first thing. I wish I could say I hop on the treadmill, but that version of me isn't consistent yet. Maybe the "work-out" version of me will show up in the next few weeks after this book is published.

To my children, I am probably the most boring person on the planet. Most days they like me. Other days I don't know anything. But kids grow up. They figure shit out. I feel as if I've given them the tools to make the choices that suit their lives. I don't get to make those choices for them. That's not how this works.

At the end of the day, I know they love me. They love my bad jokes and my attempts to cheer them up. I remember when I was the center of their little universe. I'm not anymore – and I shouldn't be. The world is waiting for them. I can't wait to see what life brings them. Cheering them on along the way. Because truth be told, my children are and will always be my favorite humans. Bar none.

Many of my friendships have shifted. Some stayed. Some faded. A very special few will always be in my life regardless if we see each other often or just when time allows.

It's a part of the everchanging cycle of this thing we call life.

Maybe I changed. I have definitely found personal growth that I am extremely proud of. That isn't a change to be criticized for; growth is beautiful.

Maybe they changed too. It doesn't matter much now.

People come and people go.

It is what it is.

You can't make people love you or like you.

So no, I can't wrap my life up in a neat box.

My story hasn't ended. It will continue until one day it doesn't.

We learn from loss – whether it's death, a friendship ending, or an ex-husband who tried to murder you. I will probably grieve those things forever. But they never stopped me. Not from my loud laugh. Not from my terrible sense of humor. Not from dancing badly in my kitchen.

Bad things will probably never stop happening. They happen to all of us. We just hope for more good than bad.

There isn't a right or wrong way to live, other than the obvious. There is only the way that is right for you.

So I will continue.

With the bad dancing.

With the plants that may or may not grow.

With learning to be a better mom with each conflict we may encounter as they grow further into their adult lives.

With dinners I photograph and laugh about years from now.

With nurturing friendships that sometimes limp along because we're all busy.

Life isn't pretty boxes.

We hope to laugh every day. We hope to find the silly moments even in times that test us.

We hope for authentic conversations without judgment. We hope that keeps the bad at bay, at least most of the time.

Life is messy and beautiful.

They coexist in places we have yet to discover. No pretty little boxes.

I'm just so glad I found the front door.

CHAPTER 70

Just Buy The Shoes

I slipped off the pink elastic band holding the box and lid together. I lifted the top and peeked inside. My breath caught as I peeled back the white paper from the first shoe. Then the other. I set them on my desk and pushed my chair back to admire them fully.

They were stunning.

They sparkled as I turned them over in my hands, tracing the rhinestone bow at the toe and the delicate strap laced in tiny stones. I had no idea why they made me feel so giddy.

Nude satin.

Sharp pointed toe.

Slingback, three-inch kitten heel with an adjustable rhinestone strap. (I cheated — that description came straight from the Amazon listing.)

A simple accessory women buy every day. Some have a huge fetish for the little things.

Closets lined with them.

Black. Brown. Red. White. Pink.

Flats. Heels. Boots. Sneakers.

At first, I couldn't figure out the strap. I actually pulled up my Amazon orders to look at the photo again.

Laughing out loud, I slid each foot in and fastened the rhinestones snug against my skin. I stood carefully.

"Please don't fall and break an ankle," I warned myself.

I haven't worn heels in years.

Strictly sneakers. Flip-flops. Flat sandals. A chunky boot now and then.

This felt new.

Reckless almost.

Exciting.

They fit like they were made for me. After a few tentative strides across my office, I knew.

I was in love.

The dogs watched with mild concern as I snapped photos of my new obsession.

"What do you think, girls? These will go perfectly with my 'goal' dress in a few months."

Macy and Pepper offered no opinion. They are dogs. Soon they returned to their beds, fully committed to napping.

But for me, this was pure freedom.

I may not have everything. No fancy title. No luxury car. No sprawling estate. What I do have is worth more.

A job that provides and satisfies. Clients who trust me enough to open their private spaces and pay me to care for them.

A dependable car that gets me where I need to go every day.

A comfortable house with more room than I could ever truly need. I can only occupy one room at a time.

It is warm.

It is clean.

It is safe.

It is home.

In this third act of my life, I can finally exhale. There are no ghosts chasing me.

And when this book is finished, the past will become what it always should have been – a chapter already written.

I bought myself new shoes today.

And somewhere between the rhinestones and the kitten heels, I realized I am in love with my life.

Because sometimes, when you've survived what you've survived…

You just buy the shoes.

CHAPTER 71

The Last Mask I Took Off Was Mine

I wanted a witness to my life. Yet I neglected to be my own. I drank instead.

With each glass I mixed and poured, ice clinking in my glass, I became a braver version of myself. Capable of stepping onto a stage and singing karaoke without hesitation, capable of telling stories without fearing judgment.

I could step into versions of myself that felt funnier, more entertaining. Versions that audiences applauded. Versions I believed were real because they were easier to live inside than my own skin.

My vodka bottle was my witness and my constant companion. We did everything together. At night, after a particularly long session where one drink became seven, it would wrap me in an endless fog, lull me to sleep, and separate my mind from my body.

There were no dreams, just emptiness and when I woke in the morning, I would simply shake it off. I would get dressed and get to work. The sooner work was over, the sooner I could return home.

Return to my friend. The vodka bottle waiting for me in the kitchen cabinet above the stove.

I would host get-togethers with friends, looking for more witnesses to my life. As a hot summer afternoon would turn into evening, light growing more dim as the minutes ticked by, my voice would grow louder.

My laugh would penetrate over everyone else sitting gathered around the fire pit. Soon, my words would slur into unrecognizable sounds and others would pick up where I left off. The stories would tumble out in a non-cohesive mess yet everyone would laugh and carry on.

Despite everyone being starkly aware, there would be no memory of this come tomorrow morning. In the end, no witnesses to my life after all. Least of all, me.

I would struggle to remember the previous evening. Many memories would be clear yet as the night had progressed, there would be less there for me to put language to. Although I see it now, after finding clarity through my sobriety, I was blind to the bigger problem.

I didn't see that it would have been most important to take a deep look at myself. Look at the person created by alcohol. Consider this might be a woman who had become terrified of being unseen. Someone who used alcohol to remove the disapproval she felt about herself.

The insecurity would vanish with each drop as it coolly slid down her throat. Glass after glass. Night after night.

It didn't matter if I had company. I didn't need a reason.

After all my grown-up duties had been ticked off the to-do-list, I would pour some of my old friend into a glass. Well, to be honest, the liquid would fill my glass as soon as I got home after an exhausting work day.

After scrubbing toilets and mopping floors, vodka was sure to lift my spirits. Boost me enough to make dinner, clean up afterwards and throw a load of clothes into the washer.

I existed in a world of rinse and repeat. Not hitting the proverbial *"rock bottom"*. That would require a reflection of myself I didn't wish to see. I would need to perform an internal inspection of what I would need to do, to stop being afraid of this woman I had become. More importantly, who she was without her trusty companion.

My fear was that I wouldn't like the person I would be without the booze. I didn't live in a constant state of impairment, so of course there were glimpses of her often. Yet, I held on so tight to the notion that I was an improvement if I had a few drinks.

I was not.

I would come to understand that I still have humor and a quick wit even though I am stone cold sober. The mask fell off finally one day, after a few days of emptying my last bottle of vodka down the drain.

I was in fact a better person, without my friend that used to live in my kitchen cupboard.

What I see now is someone who is standing in her own truth. She recognized her vulnerability, her loneliness, her desire to be the life of the party.

I am still vulnerable, but I keep myself honest by constantly checking in with myself. As far as loneliness goes, I still find myself there occasionally, but I am aware it's just a feeling I am allowing and not one that should shape my decisions.

I have still to test the *"life of the party"* theory. I consciously keep myself more reserved in large gatherings. I allow others to have a voice too.

I see myself in groups, as if looking from the outside in, and I see a softer and more kind version. Listening is a skill we learn with age. Sometimes it's kinder to hear what someone else needs to share rather than the sound of your own voice. Be a witness to someone else's life.

Even though I still miss my old friend, I don't regret dumping her into the sink. It was the only way my true self could be revealed.

These days, I don't need an audience to prove I am alive.

I don't need a glass in my hand to feel seen. The cabinet above my stove still opens and closes like it always has. Only now it holds spices, pancake syrup, baking supplies and sometimes my favorite Reese's candy bar I'm hiding from myself.

I have learned to sit quietly inside my own life and bear witness to it — the messy parts, the lonely parts, the ordinary Tuesday afternoon parts.

And for the first time, that has been enough.

CHAPTER 72

Closing The Front Door

I'm sitting on a client's front porch, taking a break from cleaning and mopping, when it hits me – there is no neat way to wrap up a life story while you're still living it. No pretty little bow. I still have a lot to do in this life I was blessed to keep. I imagine myself exploring and becoming a better version of the woman I was even yesterday.

These pages are only the beginning of what remains. We never know what comes next.

We line up dreams and goals like dominoes, but life always finds a way to knock them sideways.

I still don't know how I got here, or why I survived that summer day all those years ago. Maybe I'll never know. But not knowing doesn't change the truth: I am still here. And that is a gift.

Perhaps this belongs at the beginning of my story, but it has found its way here instead. Stories, like healing, rarely move in straight lines.

To ask what this book is about is like asking what a mirror is about – it depends on who is looking into it.

Each reader opens this book coming from their own place in the world. We all carry our own history, our own bruises and our own quiet triumphs. The same words will not land the same way twice.

They will meet you where you are, not where someone else stands.

These pages hold a journey through darkness and light.

A fight for another day and countless days after that first day of finding the front door.

My sobriety came suddenly and unexpectedly, yet it is only one part of the story. When alcohol stopped keeping the demons out and instead kept inviting them back, I knew it was time to make a change. It has awakened my soul and I am slowly returning to a place of feeling as a whole person.

There will always be harder days but I just have to remember, that only means better days are on the horizon.

This is also the story of becoming me.

I will always be flawed yet I can always work to be better. The story of a woman who once felt like a victim of her circumstances, her love, her past – and who slowly learned to gather her broken pieces and name herself something new.

Warrior. Phoenix. Survivor.

Hence the Viking-Phoenix tattoo on her left forearm.

Not because she never fell, but because she kept rising – even when climbing hurt. My story is not the only story like this.

There are many voices in the world that have cracked in the same places.

Yet if my voice can reach someone sitting in the dark, wondering if they are alone, then these words have done their job. If one person finds the courage to keep fighting, to keep getting back up and believe their life is still theirs to claim – then every page has a purpose.

We long to be seen for our strength, to wear it like armor. But true strength is not often loud. It lives in the trembling hand that still reaches for something or someone because they want to believe in the goodness in the world. It lives in the person who refuses to give up and in the tears that cleanse us, rejuvenate us rather than drown us.

What looks like weakness from the outside is often strength doing its hardest work. And, although sometimes the naked eye can't see it, it hovers quietly, bravely.

This book is an offering.

It has become a reminder to myself that I can do hard things.

If I listen close enough, there is a soft whisper that tells me, *"you are not finished yet."*

From the ashes of what was, something new can be born. I can't say that I am anyone's hero, yet I am most definitely the hero of my own survival.

Thankfully I didn't become the woman on Dateline described as *"she lit up a room."* I don't always light up a room. If ever.

I am not that special or noteworthy. But I show up as I am – forthcoming, truthful, kind, humble, loving. I try to be gentle when I can, yet fierce when I must be.

I will say since I found sobriety, I am noticeably calmer in various situations. I don't react immediately but give myself a moment to truly see the situation for what it is; nothing more and nothing less.

Am I perfect?

No, that I am not.

And, that is ok.

Perhaps I should be featured on a show like Dateline after all. Not because I was a victim who died, but because I was a victim until I wasn't.

I'm not a victim.

I am a woman who fought like hell to survive the things that happened to her. Maybe the world needs more of that. Then, the audience can decide for themselves, if I *"light up the room..."*

I am not the young girl who didn't understand what was happening to her in the years leading up to that morning all those years ago. Sometimes I think perhaps she understood more than she could bear to admit. Manipulation rarely arrives with a warning label.

Now I see her clearly. I was naive in the way young grief makes you naive. Perfect for someone who knew how to isolate her slowly – so slowly she thought the distance from friends and family was her own doing. His influence felt like love and you and I both know now that was a trap.

I ache for that twenty-something girl, so far from home that pretending felt easier than questioning.

Sometimes I want to reach back and gather her into my arms. I want to wrap her into a warm embrace and shield her in all ways possible.

I ache to peel away the bloody clothes he nearly tore from her body.

I want to gently wash the dried blood from her scalp, her feet, her trembling hands.

Like a mother would, I picture myself washing her hair gently, working shampoo through the mats until the water finally runs clear. Then I would massage the conditioner into her hair and weave my fingers softly through it to get rid of the mats.

Perhaps I would hand her a soft towel so she can take some of her power back by drying it herself. I want to take her hand and walk her forward.

Into the life waiting for her. Into motherhood. Into another marriage. And when that marriage ends too, I'd still hold her hand and say,

"keep going—your story isn't finished yet."

We glance back, because how could we not?

But then we inhale whatever comes next together.

That innocent version of me and the me of today, we merge.

Neither of us knows what the future will hold but what we do know is that now at last, we can close the front door – the one that opened in June of 1996 – and we close it together, thirty years later.

The girl and the woman become one.

Still standing.

Bloodstained no more.

CHAPTER 73

"Can We Talk?"

Remember that first question — "*Can we talk?*"

I couldn't forget it. Not because of what was asked, but because of who asked it. I turned those words over in my mind longer than I care to admit, not searching for an answer, but deciding whether this person deserved one.

In the end, it doesn't matter who.

I didn't know her.

I only knew of her.

What lingers is why – why, after nearly thirty years, those words found their way back to me.

So here I am, sitting in my office late one evening, trying to finish this book and convince myself to sleep. The house is quiet. The kind of quiet that allows memories to stretch out and sit beside you whether you invite them or not. It's late. I should be sleeping.

But there are more pressing matters than sleep. A decision.

One I already know the answer to, even if part of me resists saying it out loud.

Some days I feel grounded, wise even. Other days I feel like a little girl who still wants to pick up the phone and ask her mother what to do.

Impossible.

Here I am. No longer a young woman trying to outrun fear, but a fifty-three-year-old woman who has learned that grief doesn't fade. It changes shape. It softens around the edges, but never disappears. You learn to carry it without letting it carry you.

It is not a club anyone wants to join.

It is not something we display or perform.

Grief does not exist to gain sympathy or burden others. It simply exists. And it deserves to exist without being twisted into something cruel.

We live in it. Quietly. Permanently.

Missing my parents began long before him and existed completely separate from him. It never took love away from anyone else. It never made me less capable, less strong, or less deserving. It's just a part of my story – one thread woven through everything that followed.

As I type this, I lean back in my chair and feel the tightness in my neck and shoulders.

My fingers keep moving across the keyboard as I close my eyes and let myself go back there one last time. Not to relive it. Just to acknowledge that it happened.

Then I exhale.

It is over now.

I wrote it.

I said it.

All of it.

The pain. The fear. The chaos. The love. The laughter.

The survival.

I told the truth – even when it was uncomfortable, even when it forced me to see parts of myself I would rather have ignored.

And now, the story sits in front of me, finished.

For a moment, a familiar question drifts through my mind. Is there anything left to say?

I think about the years behind me. The mistakes. The lessons that arrived disguised as disasters. The people who stayed. The people who didn't.

The ways I kept moving forward even when I didn't feel strong enough to take another step.

I have lived imperfectly, but honestly. I have loved fiercely, sometimes recklessly, but always sincerely. And I continue, day by day, to become someone stronger, softer, wiser, and more certain of her own worth.

And through everything, my children remained my greatest proof that love can grow after devastation. I dared to love again, thus creating them.

They are kind, intelligent, compassionate adults – proof that a beautiful life can still grow after someone tries to shatter it to pieces. I love you kids, more than I can ever fully explain. More than that, I like you; you are both someone I love to spend time with.

So… have I made a decision about the question asked by a stranger?

Yes.

I knew the answer long before I allowed myself to say it out loud.

I can't talk.

There is nothing between us that requires conversation. No healing waiting to be shared. I can't offer you the answers you are likely looking for. I learned the hard way that sometimes the only answer is leaving.

Running saved my life.

Fear no longer gets a seat at my table.

I do not owe my voice to anyone.

I do, however, wish you something I once had to learn on my own – the strength to face what is right in front of you and the courage to choose a different future.

But I will not walk that road with you.

This book became the place where I said everything that needed to be said – where I finally stopped carrying silence like it was my responsibility.

This is me taking my life back.

Not loudly.

Not dramatically.

I wrote the book.

I told the story. I survived the ending he tried to write for me. And now, I get to decide what happens next.

I sit quietly for a moment, staring at the screen, letting the weight of that truth settle into something steady and familiar.

Not triumph.

Not anger.

Something calmer.

Something stronger.

Maybe it's peace?

Frankly…

He never deserved me at all.

I hover over the keyboard, rereading the message one last time. My fingers move before doubt can speak.

I close the message.

I shut the screen.

The room goes quiet.

I push back from my desk, turn off the light, and walk out of the room.

EPILOGUE

What Happens Now?

My hand hovers over the mouse as my eyes linger a moment longer on the words glowing on the computer screen in front of me.

"It's time for sleep,"

I think as the clock in the lower right corner reads 1:43 AM.

With hesitation, I push my chair back and stand to leave.

"What possibly more do you have to write?"

I ask out loud to my empty office. The dogs, curled on their beds, certainly won't have an answer.

I move through the kitchen, turning off lights as I go, making sure Macy and Pepper follow. Ozzy, the cat, is half way up the stairs already while Zoey, our other cat, is curled up in the kitchen windowsill.

My mind keeps spinning.

"Why is this so difficult? To close this chapter for good and then write about something else..."

My thoughts trail off as I check the front door. Locked, of course. Walking upstairs to my bedroom, a dull pain pulses in my left knee. My shoulders feel tight. I am exhausted.

Physically and emotionally. I have been pushing myself too hard this past month and a half. Burning the candle at both ends.

Cliché. Still true.

I begin my nighttime routine. The dogs happily hop onto the bed, settling in for sleep. Part of me wants to skip my shower, but I need the solitude it offers. As I step in and let the hot water rush over me, I breathe in.

Instinctively, I close my eyes, lean my head back, and push my hair from my face. I exhale hard. It feels like I have been holding that breath longer than I realized.

The bathroom is lit only by the glow from the open door and the light on in my walk-in closet. No need for bright lights as I sit on the shower bench that has been there since my surgery nearly three years ago. I don't need it anymore, yet I haven't been able to remove it.

It was sweet of my daughter to order it and have it delivered while I was recovering from an emergency appendectomy. It changed a lot for me.

Not the chair.

The surgery.

I had been in pain for a long time, ignoring it until I couldn't anymore. Pressure wrapped around my midsection, bringing nausea and likely a fever. Once in the ER, after a few tests, it didn't take long for the doctor to deliver the diagnosis.

"Well, young lady, guess who is the lucky winner of acute appendicitis?"

"Me?" I mused.

"Well, it isn't me. We've scheduled you for emergency surgery this evening as soon as an operating room opens," he said, attempting humor. He then noticed the tumbler beside me and frowned.

"What do you have there? Water? No water. Nothing."

"Water… and okay, no water," I answered apologetically as he left to find a nurse to move me to pre-op.

Thinking back to that day, I always return to what happened earlier, before the doctor delivered the news.

That was when I made a pinky promise with my daughter.

As they were taking down information like they always do, one of the questions was *"Do you drink alcohol?"*

"Yes, probably too much," I answered without hesitation.

My daughter was sitting in the chair to my left, while the male nurse was entering information on a tablet. He looked up.

"How much is too much? Do you drink every day?"

"Yes. Pretty much every day after work." I answered honestly.

"Mom, will you stop drinking?"

My daughter's voice chimed in to my left. I turned and looked at her. My mind was reeling and I was also feeling the effects of the morphine they had given me for the pain.

I searched my girl's face and in that moment, I knew what my answer needed to be. It was time to say goodbye to the friend who waited for me every evening in the cabinet above the stove – my vodka bottle.

"Yes, I can do that," I said.

"Do you pinky swear, Mom?"

She pushed her right pinky finger towards my left one. As they locked together, I looked at my youngest child — in her twenties, no longer a child — and said, *"I pinky promise."*

I have not had a drink since.

I allow my body to relax as the hot water continues to envelop me. I tilt my head down, noticing my hot pink toenails and the tattoos along my left arm and shoulder.

My fingers gently trace the Viking woman transformed into a phoenix across my forearm, and I smile into the dim room. I am proud of this tattoo. It holds so much — my heritage, courage, strength, my fall and rise from the ashes.

Me, becoming the woman I have grown into. Still flawed. Still searching. Still trying.

Plagued with shortcomings, yet figuring out who she truly wants to be.

The water grows too hot, and I turn the knob slightly to cool it down. Steam fills the room as I linger longer than I should, my mind refusing rest.

My eyes drift to the lion tattoo on my upper shoulder and I almost laugh.

"I never imagined I would end up with so many tattoos," I think to myself.

Each one holds a story – of what was, what is, and what may still come.

Reluctantly, I shut off the water and wrap my body in a white terrycloth robe. I twist a towel around my hair after a quick dry. As

I rub lotion into my legs and arms, chest and stomach and finally wipe any remnants of make-up off my face with my cleanser, I know sleep will not be likely to come soon.

I still have more to say. If not now, when?

I walk back downstairs through the quiet hum of the refrigerator and the dishwasher finishing its final rinse. I return to my office.

My hand wiggles the mouse and my computer screen flickers awake before my tired eyes.

2:11 AM glares at me from the bottom of the screen.

I have spent my life trying to overcome, persevere, care for others, or simply keep moving. Now, nearly thirty years after my first husband tried to murder me, after raising two incredible humans, I find myself wondering what is there left to do. What comes next?

I would like to believe I have something to offer a partner. The thought excites me – and terrifies me.

I am still navigating sobriety.

The old friend I relied on, my vodka bottle, no longer sits in my kitchen cupboard waiting to catch me when I fall.

If I allow someone new into my life, that promise must remain absolute. There is no wiggle room. Not now. I know I am not ready for an occasional glass of wine with dinner or a margarita at a Mexican restaurant. Some days, I imagine it might be possible.

But.

The word arrives immediately.

I fear finding someone who enjoys drinking and slipping back into old habits. I don't want that, however tempting it may sound. Does that mean I am meant to stay alone forever?

I don't know.

Being single has been a choice. My bed is empty except for the dogs and cat. Familiar. Easy. Safe.

I use as many pillows as I want. I can hog the blankets on cold winter nights and sleep nude on steamy summer ones. I don't know if I want to share a bed again with someone who may or may not try to control me.

Of course, I will always be a mom, no matter how old my children become. But motherhood evolves. They no longer need me to kiss scraped knees or be the finder of missing socks.

They don't need me to cut the crust off their peanut butter and jelly sandwiches. They can peel their own oranges and scoop out the stem of a strawberry with a spoon. Without my help.

Motherhood has defined my life in ways I will always be grateful for. Over the years, I would like to think I have gained patience as we navigated new challenges. I aim to listen more and speak less as they share their lives with me.

My son and daughter will always be my greatest blessings.

But they don't need me in the same way anymore. And that leaves me asking, once again, "*now what?*"

I like to call this next phase my third act.

It sounds exciting, doesn't it?

I still have no idea what it means.

Do I travel? Start a new hobby? Do I continue writing after the last period is placed at the end of this memoir? I have already started writing a psychological thriller novel. So, that's an option I muse to myself.

I hope I learn to navigate this third act. I survived violence in my twenties. I worked relentlessly to pay bills and provide for my children as they were growing up. I built confidence from ashes.

What is my identity today, nearing fifty-four, after decades of being strong, needed, and constantly in motion?

I hope silence does not unsettle me. I don't want to live trapped in my past, unable to build a future.

Saying goodbye to this project – this labor of love and heartbreak – feels terrifying. To not have this manuscript waiting on me, night after night, feels like another abandonment. Yet, in my logical mind, I know this is not true.

There are many books I never want to finish. When that last line on the final page stares back at you, there is a sense of despair that is hard to explain. You can almost feel the loneliness that comes with an ending.

Of course, it must end. I am searching for the courage to say goodbye. Perhaps that is why I am sitting here in the middle of the night. Not wanting it to end.

The clock now reads 3:17 AM.

My eyes squint against the glow of the screen, filled with black letters, words, and sentences.

"*Have you said it all now?*" I whisper.

The silence in my office lingers at that moment, less the quiet stream of piano music coming from Alexa sitting nearby. I hold the question for a moment before letting my fingers continue over the keys.

None of us knows what tomorrow holds. I cannot fear what was, and I cannot fear what comes next. With age comes clarity.

It becomes easier to see through the bullshit.

The relationship I have built with myself through writing this story is something I must trust will carry me forward. The emotional intelligence I have gained through words – through this deep excavation of my life – must be for something.

Turns out, those six months was enough. Or perhaps it's seven since I made that internal promise to myself after my last visit to the Lonestar state and my best friend. Funny how passing through an open door of an airplane can push you to break through all the barriers keeping you stuck. I am not stuck any longer.

I have to say goodbye to yesterday. Carry a few gifts with me.

And then leap.

I have to trust I will land.

Somewhere safe.

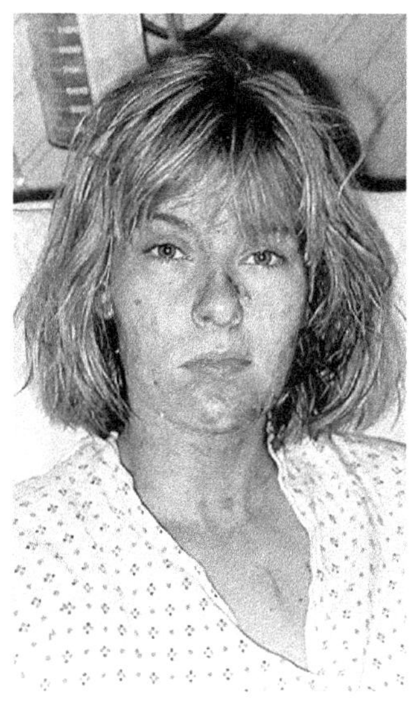

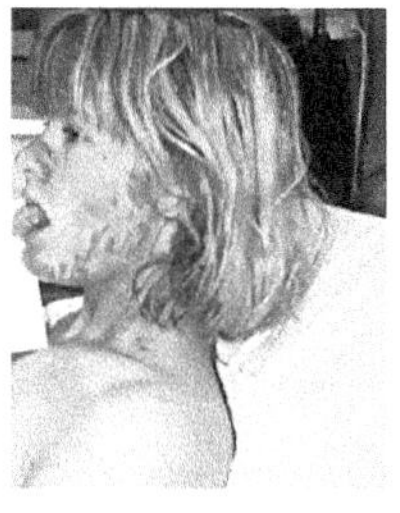

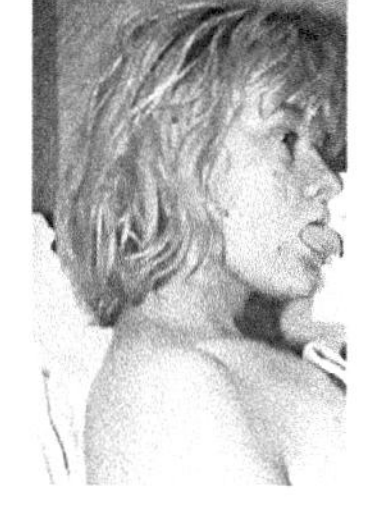

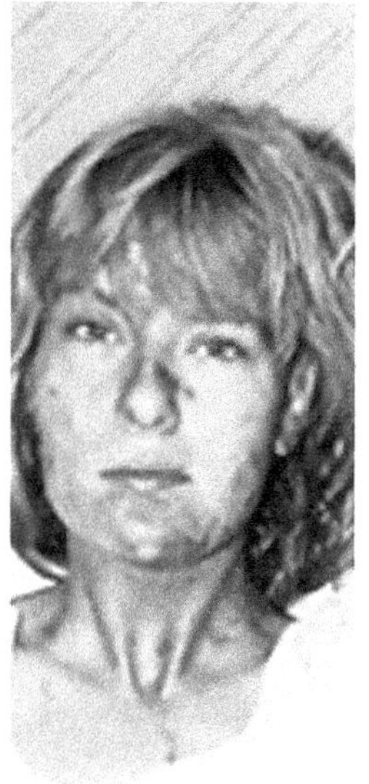

These photographs hold a version of me that existed in the shadow of violence. They captured a young woman bruised, shaken, and barely beginning to understand how close she came to losing her life when her estranged husband tried to take it. I haven't looked at these images for years as they were lost in a box stored in my garage. These photos are not a portrait of my ending – they are the evidence of my survival, and of the long, determined journey that has carried me far beyond this moment.
Author: Hjordis Madsen

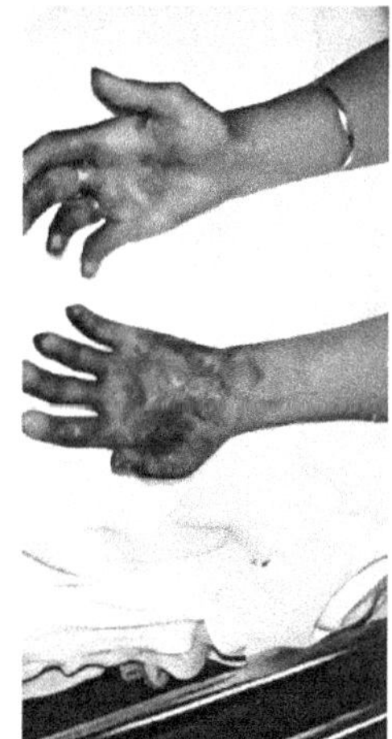

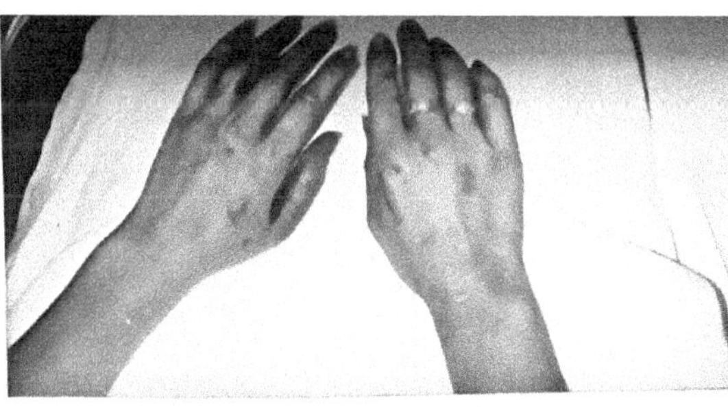

www.ingramcontent.com/pod-product-compliance
Lightning Source LLC
LaVergne TN
LVHW020705110826
845149LV00012B/2118

* 9 7 9 8 9 9 5 2 7 6 1 0 4 *